nifty notes

on
John B. Keane's
Sive

by
Aoife O'Driscoll

FOR LEAVING CERTIFICATE
ORDINARY AND HIGHER LEVEL

educate.ie

educate.ie

PUBLISHED BY:
Educate.ie
Walsh Educational Books Ltd
Castleisland, Co. Kerry, Ireland
www.educate.ie

EDITOR:
Adam Brophy

DESIGN:
The Design Gang, Tralee

PRINTED AND BOUND BY:
Walsh Colour Print, Castleisland

Copyright © Aoife O'Driscoll 2012

Sive copyright: © The Estate of John B Keane, 1986. Reprinted with kind permission of Mercier Press, Ireland

Without limiting the rights under copyright, this book is sold subject to the condition that it shall not, by way of trade or otherwise, be lent, resold, hired out, reproduced, stored in or introduced into a retrieval system, or transmitted, in any form or by any means (electronic, mechanical, photocopying, recording or otherwise), or otherwise circulated, without the publisher's prior consent, in any form other than that in which it is published and without a similar condition, including this condition, being imposed on the subsequent publisher.

IMAGES –
Druid Theatre 2003 production images, page 44 and elsewhere: © Valerie O'Sullivan; John B. Keane portrait, page 11: © Brendan Landy – Landyphoto.com; Saving turf, page 14: © Ned Moore. Other images courtesy of Stockbyte/Getty, BigStock, Sealink

The author and publisher have made every effort to trace all copyright holders. If any have been overlooked we would be happy to make the necessary arrangements at the first opportunity.

ISBN: 978-1-908507-87-7

Acknowledgements

I would like to thank everyone at Educate.ie for their help and support, particularly Adam Brophy for his wonderfully constructive advice, patience and encouragement during the writing process. I would also like to thank Janette Condon for her practical and helpful suggestions, Peter Malone for overseeing the work, and the design team for creating such a visually pleasing book.

Dedication

This book is dedicated to Conor, Niamh and Killian.

Aoife O'Driscoll

CONTENTS

Introduction 7
The Scoop 8

1 Historical Background, Summary and Analysis 13

2 Character Analysis 47

3 The Single Text 75

4 The Comparative Study 105

Glossary 164

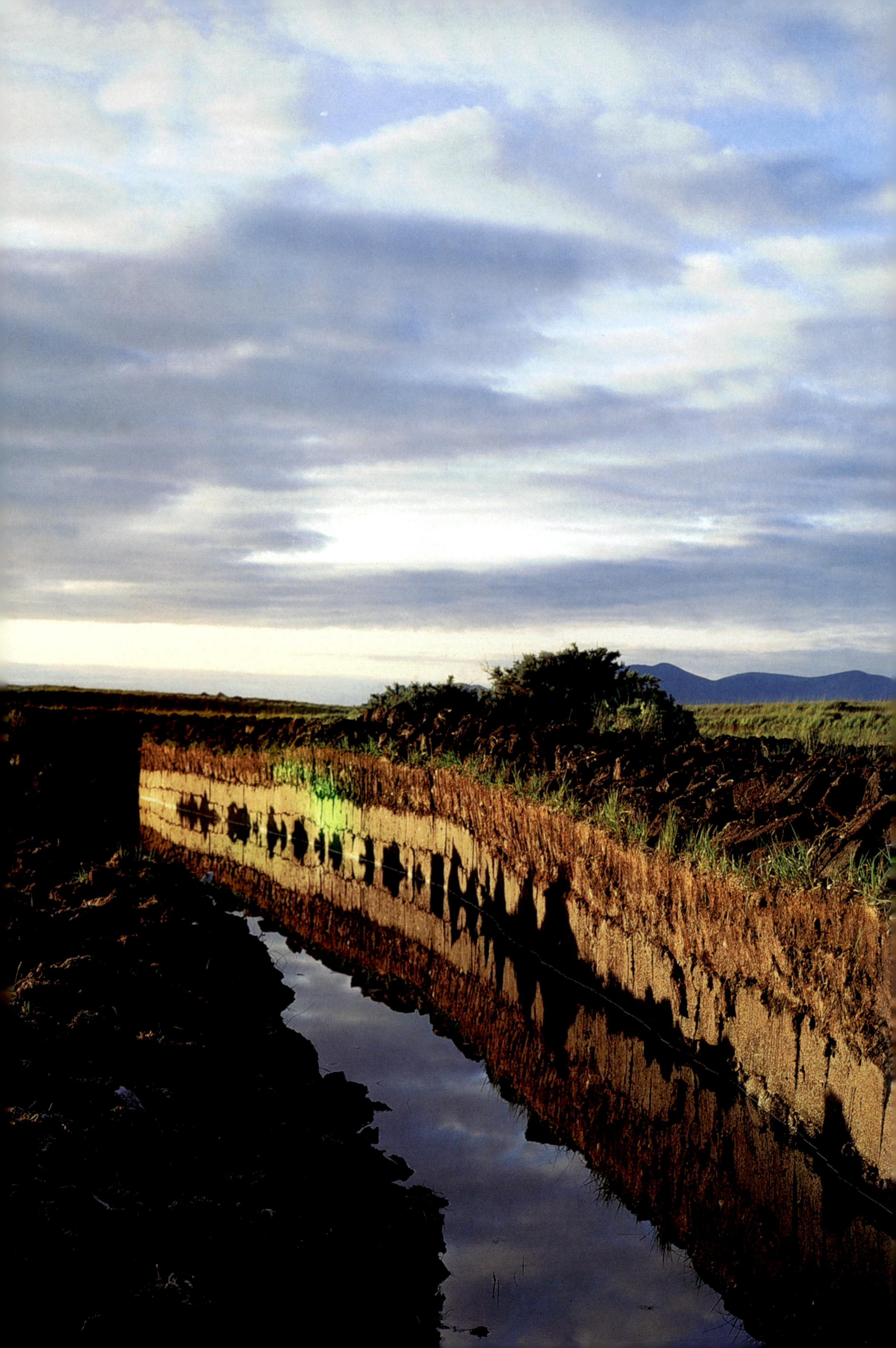

INTRODUCTION

Whether you are studying *Sive* as a Single Text or as part of your Comparative Study, you will find notes to help you in this book.

Here you will find a detailed summary and analysis of the plot, as well as in-depth character sketches, notes on each of the comparative modes for Ordinary Level and Higher Level, and a step-by-step guide (including sample answers) on how to approach this play as a Single Text.

These notes will support your reading of the play itself, where you will find the full richness of *Sive's* drama, character and language.

There runs a crisscross pattern of small leaves
Espalier, in a fading summer air,
And there Ophelia walks, an azure flower,
Whom wind, and snowflakes, and the sudden rain
Of love's wild skies have purified to heaven.

~ *Ophelia*, Walter de la Mare

the scoop

Title
The name of the play is taken from its tragic heroine.

Setting
All of the action of the play takes place in the Glavins' kitchen. The Glavins live on a remote, boggy mountain farm in the south of Ireland.

Time
1950s. The opening scene takes place in the 'late evening of a bitter March day'. The action of the play spans about three weeks.

Plot summary
Sive is a beautiful young orphan living on a poor hill farm with her uncle Mike, his wife Mena and her grandmother Nanna. Mena resents Sive because the young girl is still attending school rather than working on the land as Mena did at her age.

A local matchmaker, Thomasheen Seán Rua, comes to Mena with a proposal. An elderly farmer, Seán Dóta, wants to marry Sive and is willing to pay handsomely for the match. Seán Dóta is interested in Sive because of her youth and beauty, but he neither knows her nor loves her. A young carpenter, Liam Scuab, genuinely loves Sive, and she him. However, Sive's uncle Mike disapproves of Liam because it was Liam's cousin who fathered

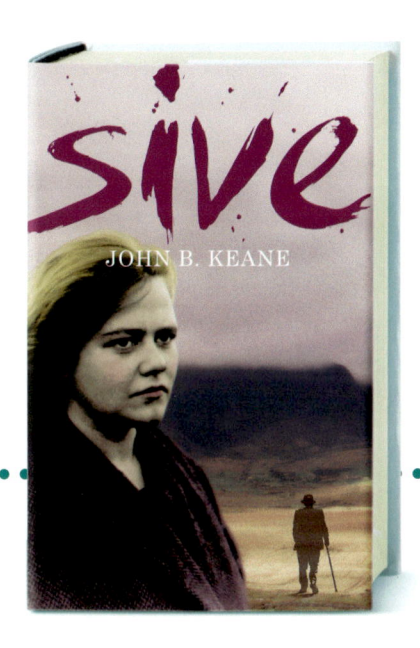

Sive, even though he and Sive's mother were not married.

Mena and Thomasheen contrive to arrange the match, and bully Sive and Mike into going along with their plan. Mena and Thomasheen are very eager to make money from the match, although Mike is less keen and worries that he is doing the wrong thing by Sive. However, he does not have the strength of will to stand up to his wife on this matter. Nanna does not agree with the match but is helpless to stop it. Mena and Thomasheen intimidate and threaten her, and Mena separates her from Sive so that the girl is isolated and more under Mena's control than ever.

The day before the wedding, Liam contrives to have a letter delivered to Nanna, to be given to Sive. In it, Liam tells Sive how much he loves her and asks her to elope with him that night. However, Nanna gives the letter to her son and asks him to pass it on. It is, in turn, intercepted by Thomasheen, who burns it.

Sive never learns that Liam is waiting for her and loves her still. She is so distraught at the thought of the marriage that she takes her own life the night before the wedding.

Themes

While there are many themes in *Sive*, some of the most commonly explored are **escape, love and marriage, isolation, corruption, the inescapable past.**

THE SCOOP

The author

- John B. Keane (1928 – 2002) was born and raised in Listowel, County Kerry. While he is perhaps best remembered for his plays, John B. Keane also wrote novels, essays, short stories and poems.

Keane and his wife bought a pub in Listowel in 1955, and it was there that he met many characters who were to provide him with inspiration for his writing. In the introduction to the Mercier Press edition of *Sive*, John B. Keane's daughter Joanna briefly tells the fascinating true story behind the play.

Sive was first performed in 1959 by the Listowel Drama Group. The play quickly became a great success and established John B. Keane as a writer.

'It [Sive] showed rural Ireland for what it really was. A wonderful place in many ways, but in many other ways a rough, tough station. Poverty was paramount, where cruelty was part of everyday life, where people only barely survived'

John B. Keane interview, 1998

© BRENDAN LANDY - LANDYPHOTO.COM

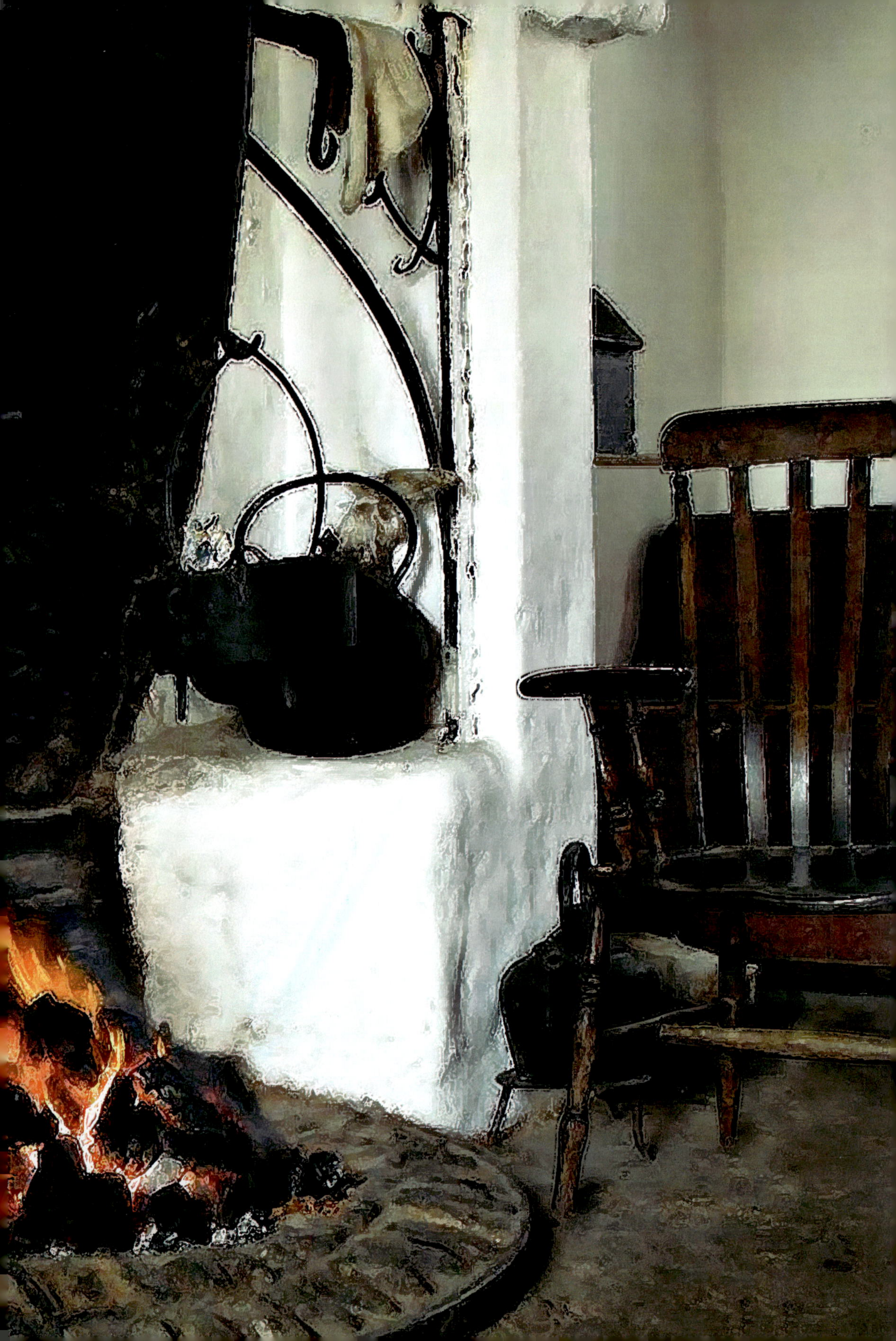

Historical background, summary and analysis

1

HISTORICAL BACKGROUND

Poverty and progress in the 1950s

Ireland in the 1950s was a country struggling with poverty and high levels of emigration. After over thirty-five years of independence, many people were still not seeing the benefits of separation from Britain. Life was hard, and over half a million people emigrated in the decade from 1950 to 1960. This is referenced in *Sive*, when we hear that Sive's father went to Britain to seek work in the hope that he would be able to earn enough to make a home for Sive's mother. With so many young people leaving the country, the population was weighted in favour of older people. Consequently, there was a tendency for society to remain conservative and unwilling to accept new ways of thinking.

However, there were signs of change, even in the midst of the economic gloom. One of the side effects of emigration was that there was less competition for jobs and resources among those who stayed at home. At the same time, there was a drive towards foreign investment and away from the traditional monopoly of the wealthy dynasties that had controlled a large part of the country's businesses. Ordinary Irish people at last had the chance to make money for

Hauling turf from the bog. As well as burning it at home, farmers sold the fuel to raise much-needed cash

themselves and to better themselves socially. Mention is made of this in *Sive* when Pats Bocock tells Mena: 'There is money-making everywhere. The face of the country is changing.'

The play is an accurate reflection of the change from the old Ireland to the new. Economic pressure leads Mena to jump at the chance of a match which would bring her £200, and even Mike admits that the money is 'a great temptation'. Both are mindful of the constant threat of poverty and both are keen to leap on the chance of an increase in income. Sive and Liam, on the other hand, reflect the new Ireland and the hope for a better future. For the young couple, love and personal happiness is more important than financial security. For Mena, and to a lesser extent Mike, financial security is paramount. The moral dilemma that results from the division between modern values and the traditional customs of a dying past is at the heart of this tragic play.

A more detailed description of the historical background of *Sive* can be found in the Comparative Study section of this book, under the heading 'Cultural Context/Social Setting' (page 120).

In the 1950s tens of thousands of young Irish people took the emigration boat to Britain every year

SUMMARY AND ANALYSIS

Act 1, Scene 1

The setting is an Irish country kitchen, simply and traditionally furnished. There is little evidence of wealth or modernity, even by 1950s standards. The cooking is done over an open fire and there is no running water.

Nanna Glavin, 'mother of the man of the house', sits by the fire, surreptitiously smoking a pipe and idly tending the fire. She seems not to have much to do and is merely killing time. Nanna is dressed in the traditional style of elderly countrywomen of that era: black skirts with a heavy red petticoat underneath and long, laced boots. When she hears the door opening, Nanna hurriedly hides the pipe under her skirts.

Mena, Mike's wife, enters. She is in her early forties, strong and 'hard-featured'. Her hair is pulled back severely and tied into a bun. The overall impression Mena gives is of someone tough and unyielding.

Mena's first words are an accusation; she rightly suspects that Nanna has been smoking. Nanna claims the smell is merely burning turf and hastily pokes the fire in an effort to increase the smoke and thus hide the smell of tobacco. Mena sets to work preparing a bucket of animal feed and the two women continue their hostile conversation. Nanna bemoans the fact that her home has been made so unhappy by her nagging daughter-in-law, and rather cruelly says that Mena should have three or four children by now. Mena responds by saying that she could have made a better marriage for herself, and speaks scornfully of her husband and his farm, saying that if it weren't for her they would be in a far worse state. Nanna is equally contemptuous of Mena's father and her family's poverty. There is no love lost between these two women.

As Mena goes to leave, Sive enters. She is a pretty young girl of eighteen, rather poorly dressed in an ill-fitting coat over her school uniform. Sive explains that she is late home because her bicycle got a puncture. The schoolmaster gave her a lift part of the way home. Mena is unsympathetic and says that she hopes Sive does not expect her to have dinner ready. Sive's reply, that she ate 'fricassée with dartois' which she and the other girls made during cookery class, does not please Mena, who snaps that Sive has 'high notions' and should be out working on a farm. As she leaves the kitchen, Mena hints darkly that Sive will come to no good, like 'the one that went before' her.

Sive realises that Mena is referring to her late mother and turns to Nanna for an explanation. Nanna is reluctant to elaborate, saying that Sive shouldn't listen to Mena's poisonous talk. Sive urges Nanna to tell her more, saying that all she knows about her parents is that her mother died when she was a baby, and that her father drowned. Nanna is clearly uncomfortable with the direction the conversation is taking, and will only say that Sive's father was drowned in a coal-mining accident in England shortly after Sive's birth. She admits that Sive's mother was pretty, 'too pretty'. Although Sive is eager to hear all about her mother, Nanna wants to change the subject, claiming that there is no more to tell. It is obvious that there is some mystery surrounding Sive's parents.

At that moment, Mena re-enters the kitchen, unnoticed by Sive or

SUMMARY AND ANALYSIS

Nanna. She hears them discussing Sive's mother for a moment or two before Nanna notices her and warns Sive with a glance.

Mena immediately begins to berate Sive for lazing about while she and Sive's uncle work hard to provide for her. She turns on Nanna too, pointing out that if she continues to hide her pipe under her skirts she will catch fire some day. Nanna lashes back by wishing that if such a thing were to happen she would manage to set fire to Mena at the same time. She claims that Mena would burn easily as she is so dry and barren. Once again, she taunts her daughter-in-law about her infertility. Mena's reply, that at least she didn't have a child out of wedlock, is clearly meant as a jibe about Sive's mother. She orders the girl to her room to study and then turns on Nanna, accusing her of filling Sive's head with nonsense. Mena makes it obvious that she resents the fact that Sive does not have to do any physical labour and is, unlike Mena at her age, allowed to stay in school rather than earn her living on a farm. She and Nanna exchange a few more unpleasant words before Nanna follows Sive into her room.

Alone in the kitchen, Mena busies herself with some household tasks. There is a knock on the door, and Thomasheen Seán Rua, the matchmaker, enters. He is a shabby, sly-looking man of around forty. He asks if Mena is alone and it is clear that he has something confidential to discuss with her. He makes small talk about farming and the weather, but Mena is impatient, telling him to get to the point. He does so, saying that he has come on behalf of a man who wants to marry Sive. Mena is astonished that anyone would want to make a match with an illegitimate schoolgirl. Thomasheen assures her that there is such a suitor, but it appears that the man is old and that it is Sive's youthful beauty alone that has attracted him. He tells Mena that the man is Seán Dóta, a well-off farmer. Mena protests that he is 'as old as the hills', but Thomasheen says that he still wants a young wife. Sive will live a life of luxury, Thomasheen tells Mena, and he further sweetens the deal by saying that, far from wanting a dowry, Seán Dóta is willing to pay Mena two hundred sovereigns if the marriage goes ahead. (At the time this would have been a substantial amount, the equivalent of the price of a new car.)

Mena has doubts about Sive's willingness to co-operate and Thomasheen suggests that she bully and threaten Sive into agreeing. When Mena says that this may only make matters worse as Sive is 'flighty like a colt', Thomasheen changes tack and encourages her to entice Sive with sweet words and promises of a life of luxury with an old man who is not likely to live more than another year or two. When Mena worries aloud that Nanna will put a stop to the match, Thomasheen comes up with the idea of making it part of the deal that Nanna move to Sive's new home with her. Mena is pleased at that thought, reflecting that she would be rid of a mother-in-law she detests and a step-daughter she resents.

Mena's last doubt about the proposed match is how her husband, Mike, will react to the news. Thomasheen seems confident that she will be able to talk Mike around. He speaks seriously for a moment, telling Mena

> Mena has doubts about Sive's willingness to co-operate and Thomasheen suggests that she bully and threaten Sive into agreeing

that married couples are fortunate to have one another and that he knows what it is to be lonely. He believes that Mena and Mike have 'the one will' between them and that their closeness will enable her to bring him around to her way of thinking. Reverting back to his normal manner, he reminds her again of the two hundred sovereigns and says that he and Seán Dóta will call that night, as if by chance.

Nanna comes into the kitchen to get a cup of milk for Sive, and is not pleased to see Thomasheen there. She tells him that she is sure he is up to no good. He does not reply, but as soon as she leaves the room he curses her and tells Mena that she will do well to be rid of the old woman.

Mena hears Mike coming back from the village and hastily ushers Thomasheen out.

Mike has sold a couple of piglets for a good sum of money, which he

SUMMARY AND ANALYSIS

hands over to Mena. He is pleased with the price he received for the animals, telling his wife that things are looking up for small farmers at last. Money is important to Mike Glavin and he is delighted not to be scrimping and saving as much as he used to.

Mena broaches the subject of the match for Sive. She does not mention the man's name, but focuses on his wealth. Mike cannot imagine any prosperous farmer wanting to marry a girl without a fortune of her own. He is also dubious about Sive's willingness to agree to a match as she has been well educated and will want to make her own choices. He reminds Mena that Sive is young and that he promised his late sister he would look after the girl. Mena is scornful, saying that it is not his fault that his sister died, or that she was 'too free with men'. Mike reacts angrily to this criticism of his sister but Mena is unrepentant. She says Sive's illegitimacy means that she is highly unlikely to get a better chance than this. Mike remains doubtful.

When Mena reveals the name of the suitor, Mike's doubt changes to fury and disgust. He vows that the match will never take place and wonders how Mena could even consider such a thing. The mention of the two hundred sovereigns does nothing to placate Mike, who refuses to consider sacrificing an innocent girl to a 'corpse of a man'. Mena scorns him for his weakness and he storms out of the house, saying that he wants to be alone. She follows him, calling his name.

Nanna comes back into the empty kitchen and takes up her position by the fire, smoking her pipe. As she does so, a handsome young man of nineteen enters. He is Liam Scuab.

Liam marvels aloud at all the commotion he has seen: first Thomasheen sneaking away from the house, then Mike storming out, followed by Mena.

Nanna warns him that he will be in trouble if he is caught in the house and Liam replies that he has only called in for a few moments to talk to Sive. Nanna calls the girl. Sive is surprised and pleased to see him but worries that her aunt and uncle will find him there. Nanna leaves them alone together but advises them to keep watch.

The young lovers make a plan to meet secretly later that night. Liam mentions having seen Thomasheen Seán Rua leaving the house and Sive wonders what 'that devil' wanted. She and Liam discuss matchmaking, agreeing that it is a dreadful custom. While Liam acknowledges that there are people who see the value of matchmaking in rural areas, he says that the only person he would consider marrying is Sive.

Sive tells Liam that he should leave before he is caught, but it is too late. Mike Glavin comes in and is furious to see Liam Scuab in his kitchen. He sends Sive to her room and rounds on Liam, accusing him of being up to no good with his niece. Liam tells Mike that his intentions are honest and that he loves Sive, but Mike is unimpressed. He compares Liam to his cousin, Sive's father, who left Sive's mother when she fell pregnant. Liam defends his cousin, saying that he did not know Sive's mother was pregnant when he left for England and that he was drowned before he could come home and marry her.

KEY QUESTIONS

- From what you have read so far, what do you think are the main sources of conflict between Nanna and Mena?
- Why does Mike think Sive should not marry Seán Dóta?
- Why do you think Mike does not want Liam Scuab to go out with Sive? Do you agree with his assessment of Liam?
- Why do you think Thomasheen approaches Mena rather than Mike? What does this choice tell us about Thomasheen's character?

WRITING TASK

- In what way would you say that Nanna, Mena and Sive represent different generations of Irish women? In your answer you may wish to consider some of the following: clothing, habits, work, position in the family, education, attitude to marriage and children.

SUMMARY AND ANALYSIS

❝ Important quotations

Nanna to Mena	'Fitter for you to be having three or four children put from you at this day of your life'
Mena to Sive	'Out working with a farmer you should be, my girl, instead of getting your head filled with high notions'
Mena to Nanna	'Some day that pipe will take fire where you have it hidden and you'll go off in a big black ball of smoke and ashes'
Nanna replying to Mena's comment above	'If I do, 'tis my prayer that the wind will blow me in your direction and I'll have the satisfaction of taking you with me'
Thomasheen to Mena, advising her how to make Sive agree to the match	'Isn't she a bye-child? Tell her you will bell-rag her through the parish if she goes against you. Tell her you will hunt the oul' woman into the county home'
Mena to Thomasheen, referring to young people like Sive	''Tis all love and romancing these days with little thought for comfort or security'
Thomasheen to Mena, referring to Seán Dóta	'How many years have he spent searchin' the country for a young woman?'
Mena to Thomasheen, explaining how she will persuade Mike to agree to the match	'I will come around himself in my own time. He has a great love for the few pounds'
Mike to Mena	'Money is the best friend a man ever had'
Mike to Mena, talking about Sive	'When my sister died I gave my word that I would stand by her. The girl is too young. She has no father. I have responsibility'
Mike to Mena, saying why he cannot agree to Sive's marrying Seán Dóta	'It would be like tossing the white flower of the canavaun on to the manure heap'

'Who will take her with the slur and the doubt hanging over her?'	Mena to Mike, talking about Sive
'Would you marry somebody you never saw before?'	Sive to Liam, as they discuss matchmaking
'I would marry nobody but you, Sive, I love you. How would I marry anybody but you!'	Liam to Sive
'I know your breed, Scuab, and what you are and I know what you're looking for'	Mike to Liam
'Quick words and book-readin' like all belonging to you'	Mike to Liam
'You will not command the lives and happiness of two young people who love each other'	Liam to Mike

Act 1, Scene 2

It is now nightfall. Sive, Mike and Mena are in the kitchen. All are busy. Sive is studying, Mike is mending an old, worn harness, and Mena is washing a shirt by hand. Mike and Mena's tasks show us how hard they have to work, day and night, in order to eke out a living on their poor farm, while Sive's studying seems to indicate that her life is destined to follow a different path.

Mena seems to be awaiting the arrival of a visitor. Moments later, Thomasheen Seán Rua and Seán Dóta appear. Seán Dóta is a small, wrinkled, elderly man with a self-effacing manner. Thomasheen makes a great show of pointing out Seán Dóta's positive attributes, claiming that he is fit, healthy, easy-going and very pleasant. Seán Dóta nods in agreement but also tries to appear modest. Seán Dóta's physical appearance, and his habit of giving a half laugh as if to apologise for everything he says, are unappealing and do not match up to Thomasheen's flattering description of him. Although Mena welcomes the visitors, Mike does not seem as impressed. Nevertheless he offers

SUMMARY AND ANALYSIS

them tea, which both men refuse. Thomasheen turns his attention to Sive, asking what she is studying. When she replies that she is reading poetry, Thomasheen launches into a poem advising young girls to avoid young men. It is quite obvious that he is trying to introduce the idea of an older man being a better prospect for a woman. He draws Seán Dóta into the conversation and asks what he thinks of poetry. Seán Dóta's answer, that all poets are 'filled with roguery' and are 'thieves' is unlikely to endear him to the studious Sive. However, at Thomasheen's urging, Seán Dóta recites a poem in an effort to impress Sive. It is a nonsensical children's rhyme and could not possibly appeal to an educated young woman like Sive. Mena, Mike and Thomasheen pretend to be delighted by the recitation.

Mena, speaking in a far kinder manner than we have heard so far, asks Sive to go on an errand to a house at the end of the road. Sive agrees, reluctantly. Mena takes the opportunity to tell everyone present how helpful Sive is. Thomasheen pretends that he has to go home by a different route, but suggests that Seán Dóta accompany Sive on her short journey. Sive says she does not need company or protection, and scorns suggestions of evil spirits walking abroad at night. Seán Dóta promises to protect Sive and tries in vain to impress her by saying that he is thinking of buying a motor car. Sive is annoyed to have to walk with the old man but has no choice but to go with him. She and Seán Dóta leave.

Thomasheen and Mena seem confident the match will be made. Mike is still very unsure, claiming that Sive is too young, intelligent and romantic to marry Seán Dóta. Mena reminds him about the money they will make from the match and about Liam Scuab's interest in Sive. Thomasheen scorns Mike's talk of romance and asks if he has ever treated Mena romantically. Thomasheen says he is sure that Mike has not and that he would be more likely to treat his pigs with affection than to show any love for his wife. Mena is stung by this and says Thomasheen is 'no one to talk'. Thomasheen agrees and, in a moment of honesty, says that he was in love once but that his father committed suicide and the money Thomasheen had saved to marry the girl had to be spent on his father's funeral instead. He recovers quickly from this moment of truth and announces cheerfully that if he is paid for this match, he will have enough to marry a local widow.

In order to manipulate Mike into agreeing to the marriage, Thomasheen tells him that Sive and Liam Scuab have been meeting secretly. Mike worries that Sive might become pregnant out of wedlock, like her mother before her. Mena suggests moving Sive to a bedroom that can only be accessed through her and Mike's bedroom. This way, Mena will be able to keep a close eye on the girl. She also warns against letting Nanna hear anything of the proposed match as she suspects that the old woman is encouraging the romance between Sive and Liam Scuab.

> In order to manipulate Mike into agreeing to the marriage, Thomasheen tells him that Sive and Liam Scuab have been meeting secretly

Thomasheen says that even that won't be enough and that Sive must be taken out of school and kept at home, lest she meet Liam Scuab on her way there or back. Mike is still unconvinced about their chances of getting Sive to marry Seán Dóta but Mena and Thomasheen are thinking greedily about the money and do not want to hear any negative comments.

With one last warning about Nanna, Thomasheen leaves. Mike says he will not wait up for Sive. It is obvious that he feels guilty about the plans they are making and does not think he could face the girl. Mena says nothing to this, but claims that she is tired too and will go with him. They leave the kitchen and Nanna enters. Satisfied that her son and daughter-in-law have gone to bed, she sits by the fire and lights her pipe.

A moment later, Sive enters. She is distressed, and tells Nanna that

SUMMARY AND ANALYSIS

Seán Dóta made a vicious pass at her and that she only escaped by running into a neighbour's kitchen. Sive is disgusted by Seán Dóta and calls him 'an ould sick thing'. She asks Nanna why the old man should have done such a thing. Nanna is unperturbed and tells Sive that it's just the way all men, old or young, behave. She dismisses the incident but Sive wonders aloud if there is a plan afoot to make a match between her and Seán Dóta. She can hardly believe such a thing would be possible, but Nanna takes her seriously and suspects Mena of colluding with Thomasheen.

Mena comes out of her room and angrily sends Sive and Nanna to bed, accusing them of gossiping and wasting lamp oil. Sive and Nanna leave the kitchen and Mena quenches the lamp.

KEY QUESTIONS

- In the first scene, Mike was suspicious of Liam Scuab and accused him of wanting to take advantage of Sive, yet in this scene, he allows Seán Dóta to walk down the road with Sive in the dark. Do you think Mike is truly concerned with protecting Sive's honour?
- How is Seán Dóta represented in this scene?
- Do you have any sympathy for Thomasheen Seán Rua? Why/why not?
- Outline the ways in which Thomasheen and Mena plan to isolate Sive from Liam and Nanna.

WRITING TASK

- Write the diary entry you think Sive might have written after the events of the evening.

❝ Important quotations

Stage directions about Seán Dóta
'Whenever he speaks he also smiles with a half-laugh as if to excuse himself'

Seán Dóta
'I have nothing against the poets, mind you, but they are filled with roguery and they have the bad tongue on top of it, the thieves'

'But think of the dark, girl, and the phuca, the mad, red eyes of him like coals of fire lighting in his head.'	Thomasheen to Sive
'There will be no one cross her path with Seán Dóta walking by her side'	Seán Dóta, offering to escort Sive down the road to a neighbour's house
'The seed is sown; the flower will blossom'	Thomasheen to Mike and Mena when Sive and Seán Dóta leave the house together
'The money is a great temptation but there is wrong in it from head to heel. Sive is young, with a brain by her. She will be dreaming about love with a young man'	Mike to Mena and Thomasheen, expressing his doubts about the match
'What I say is what business have the likes of us with love? It is enough to have to find the bite to eat'	Thomasheen to Mena and Mike
'I don't want her going the same road as her mother'	Mike expressing his fears about Sive's relationship with Liam
''Twould be a black day for us if we robbed a widow or stole a poor-box from the chapel. Isn't it only bringing two people together in wedlock we are?'	Thomasheen to Mike and Mena, explaining why he thinks they are doing nothing wrong by arranging the match
'Watch the oul' one up there! She have the makin's of trouble'	Thomasheen to Mena and Mike, warning them about Nanna
'I have no heart somehow for looking her in the face'	Mike to Mena, saying why he will not stay up until Sive comes home
'Oh, and the way he laughs, like an ould sick thing'	Sive to Nanna, expressing her revulsion for Seán Dóta

Act 1, Scene 3

It is late afternoon, one week later. Nanna and Mena are in the kitchen. Nanna is sitting by the fire, and Mena is making bread. The two women bicker and Nanna again bemoans the fact that she is without a grandchild. Mena lashes back that Nanna is 'alluding and criticising always'. She claims that children only bring sadness. She reminds Nanna that her own two children did not do well in life. Sive's mother had an illegitimate child and died soon afterwards, while Mike is a poor hill farmer, struggling to make ends meet. It is ironic that Mena should accuse Nanna of 'alluding and criticising', when she does exactly the same thing to Nanna.

Mena puts the bread on to bake and announces that she is going out to take care of the cattle. Nanna challenges her, saying that she suspects Mena of plotting to make a match between Seán Dóta and Sive. Mena reacts by scornfully pointing out that Sive is an illegitimate child and should be very grateful to have such a good match made for her. Nanna is unimpressed and accuses Mena of suiting herself. Mena curses the old woman, but before Nanna can respond, Thomasheen Seán Rua enters. He warns Mena that a pair of travelling men, Pats Bocock and his son, Carthalawn, are heading for the house. Nanna speaks favourably of the travelling men but Mena and Thomasheen think little of them.

The sounds of a bodhrán and singing signal the arrival of Pats Bocock and his son. They enter. Pats is a lame man dressed in a shabby, formal suit and hat, while his son is dressed in a similar, if somewhat less formal, fashion. As they walk in, father and son keep step with one another. This shows that there is an unspoken understanding between the two.

Pats strikes the floor with his stick and Carthalawn mimics the same rhythm on his bodhrán. They sing a song in praise of the man of the house, as is traditional. Nanna rises to show her respect. She applauds the song but Mena and

Thomasheen appear not to care about it one way or the other. Pats compliments Nanna on her good health and vigour, and praises Mena for her generosity. This is obviously in the hope that Mena will rise to the praise by giving them food or money. He goes to shake Thomasheen's hand but the other man turns away. Mena rather ungraciously asks what the pair want and Pats replies that they would be grateful for some bread and tea or some cash. He also suggests that Thomasheen may have some money to spare, as he earns so much. Thomasheen hotly denies this and suggests that Pats and his son earn their own money, particularly when there is plenty of work available for manual labourers.

Nanna warns Thomasheen that 'there is no luck in refusing a man of the road', and sure enough, Pats and Carthalawn launch into a song which curses Thomasheen for his meanness. As Carthalawn sings, Pats points his stick at Thomasheen in a rather menacing fashion.

When the song is over, Nanna says that she will give the father and son some tea and sugar, but Mena forbids her to do so. Thomasheen supports Mena in her decision, jeeringly calling Pats Bocock and Carthalawn 'the two biggest robbers walking the roads of Ireland'.

Pats and Carthalawn move towards the door. Thomasheen believes he has defeated them. He mocks Pats' lame leg and accuses Carthalawn of being 'a half-fool'.

Once again, Pats and Carthalawn launch into a song. This time the subject matter is a young girl being sold in marriage to an old man. Thomasheen and Mena exchange glances at this reference to the proposed match between Sive and Seán Dóta. Mena accuses Pats of 'hiding behind the words' of his son and tells him to speak plainly. Pats replies that everybody is gossiping about the fact that Sive is to be married to Seán Dóta, and that Thomasheen will make money from the deal.

> Pats replies that everybody is gossiping about the fact that Sive is to be married to Seán Dóta, and that Thomasheen will make money from the deal

Mena reacts defensively to the accusation, while Nanna calls the match 'devil's work'. Pats says he and his son will visit again the night before the wedding. Thomasheen says they will not be welcome and

SUMMARY AND ANALYSIS

he insults Pats and Carthalawn once again. Again, the tinkers respond with a song which mocks and insults Thomasheen. They leave the house, Carthalawn singing as they go.

Alone with Nanna, Mena and Thomasheen begin to bully her cruelly. Thomasheen accuses her of spreading gossip about the match and Mena backs him up. Together they warn Nanna that she could be turned out of the house and put into the county home. Nanna says that she will tell Mike of their threats, but Mena claims that Mike doesn't care about her. Thomasheen, showing how cunning he can be, tells Nanna a story of a woman who was sent to the county home and died in torment because she was not allowed to smoke. He knows Nanna loves her pipe and calculates that this tale will frighten her. Mena says that Nanna will never leave the comfort of a home where she is fed regularly. Nanna does not respond directly to Mena but instead says, to nobody in particular, that 'there is a hatchery of sin in this house'. Mena rounds violently on Nanna and scathingly compares her to an ungrateful child.

> Alone with Nanna, Mena and Thomasheen begin to bully her cruelly

Nanna leaps on the reference to a child and makes it clear she is sad there is no child in the house. Mena is incensed by this and threatens to strike Nanna. Thomasheen intervenes and prevents the attack. Nanna leaves, but not before repeating her comment about the house being 'a hatchery of sin'.

Mena is still furious but Thomasheen assures her that Nanna is a spent force. Age is tiring her, he claims.

The conversation turns to the match. Mena wants to know when Seán Dóta will hand over the money and Thomasheen tells her that he will only do so on the day of the wedding. Thomasheen is anxious to hear that Sive has agreed to the marriage. Mena assures him that she has the situation under control.

Mena hears Sive arriving home from school and tells Thomasheen to go and leave matters to her. Sive enters and looks displeased to see Thomasheen and Mena together. Thomasheen tries to talk to her but she ignores him and addresses Mena, telling her that the bike is punctured again. Thomasheen leaves.

To Sive's surprise, Mena is kind and considerate. She promises to get new tubes for the bike and offers Sive tea and cake. This behaviour is in stark contrast to the unsympathetic way Mena reacted in the opening scene when Sive came home with a similar story.

Mena begins to discuss the match with Sive, stressing how wealthy she will be and how happy Nanna will be to live with her in such a fine house. Sive says that she could never consider marrying Seán Dóta and that she is repulsed at the thought. Mena continues to speak in a kind tone as she assures Sive that she will come to her senses and realise how lucky she is to have the chance of escaping a future full of poverty and hard work. Sive is not won over so Mena changes tack slightly. Cunningly, she makes a reference to Sive's birth, hinting that it is part of the reason Sive should consider herself fortunate to have the opportunity to marry so well.

Mena has judged well. Sive now shows an interest in the conversation. She tells Mena that she has never been told much about her parents. Mena promises to tell Sive the story, claiming that Mike could never bring himself to do it and Nanna is 'never the one to come out with the truth'. She tells Sive that her parents were not married and that her father took advantage of her mother and then left her. Sive is bewildered, having always believed that her father drowned in England. Mena repeats that he simply disappeared and left her mother pregnant with Sive. She claims that the shame of this killed Sive's mother. Mena pretends to be kind and understanding as she tells this story, but the main point she wants to drive home is that Sive is illegitimate. To her irritation, Sive does not seem to pick up on that and asks again what Mena knows about her father. Mena's motherly manner begins to slip and she says harshly that her father was nothing more than a nameless man driven by lust and that Sive is 'a bye-child,

SUMMARY AND ANALYSIS

a common bye-child – a bastard!'

Sive tries to stand up to go but Mena pushes her back into the chair and throws her schoolbag across the room. She has dropped the kindly act now and tells Sive in no uncertain terms that she will not be going back to school any more, nor will she be sharing a room with Nanna. It is time, she says, that Sive realised she is a woman, not a girl. She tells Sive of her own desperately poor childhood and says that she and her sisters lived for the day they would find a husband to take them away from it all. Mena has no time for romance, calling it 'rameish and blather'. The most important quality in a prospective husband, she claims, is land and money. She sends Sive to her room to think about what she has said.

KEY QUESTIONS

- Why do you think Mena and Thomasheen dislike Pats Bocock and Carthalawn?
- What do you think Nanna means when she says 'There is a hatchery of sin in this house'?
- How is the tension between Mena, Thomasheen and Nanna created in this scene? You should refer to the stage directions in your answer.
- Describe the various ways in which Mena tries to persuade Sive to agree to the match.

WRITING TASK

- 'Thomasheen Seán Rua has an uncanny knack of recognising people's vulnerabilities and using them to bend others to his will.' Do you agree or disagree with this statement? Support your answer with reference to the text.

66 Important quotations

Nanna to Mena
"Tis hard enough for a lonely old woman without a child to rock in the cradle'

Mena to Nanna, referring to Sive
'Thanking me from her heart, she should be, the fine match I am making for her'

'They are people of the road – travelling people. They are above the class beggar'	Nanna to Mena and Thomasheen, referring to Pats Bocock and Carthalawn
'Carthalawn, your best! Your Almighty best!'	Pats to his son, urging him to curse Thomasheen in song
'There is no luck in refusing a man of the road'	Nanna to Thomasheen
'He's as greedy as a sow; / And the crow behind the plough, / That black man from the mountain, Seanín Rua!'	Part of Carthalawn's song about Thomasheen Seán Rua
'The people are saying that it is a strange match that a young girl who is at the start of her days should marry an old man who is at the end of his'	Pats, speaking about the match between Sive and Seán Dóta
'You are the bladder of a pig, the snout of a sow; you are the leavings of a hound, the sting of a wasp. You will die roaring'	Pats Bocock's venomous curse on Thomasheen
'You are a lone woman with your husband feeding worms in the trench. You have terrible gumption with no one left to back you'	Thomasheen to Nanna
'Little your son cares about you. Long ago you should have been put in your place'	Mena to Nanna
'There is a hatchery of sin in this house'	Nanna, addressing nobody in particular, but it is clear that she is talking about Mena and Thomasheen
'Think about the handling of thousands and the fine clothes and perfumery. Think of the hundreds of pounds in creamery cheques that will come in the door to you and the servant boy and the servant girl falling all over you for fear you might dirty your hands with work'	Mena to Sive, trying to show her the benefits of a match with Seán Dóta

SUMMARY AND ANALYSIS

Sive to Mena, begging that she not be forced to marry Seán Dóta	'Please, please … you don't know what you are saying. How can you ask me such a thing?'
Mena to Sive, trying to show her the benefits of a match with Seán Dóta	'Will you thank God that you won't be for the rest of your days working for the bare bite and sup like the poor women of these parts'
Mena to Sive	'It's time you were told, my girl. You are a bye-child, a common bye-child – a bastard!'
Mena to Sive	'Take heed of a man with a piece of property. He will stand over his promise'

Act 2, Scene 1

Mena is sitting at the table, writing a shopping list for the wedding. There is a knock at the door and Liam Scuab enters. Mena makes it clear that he is not welcome but Liam ignores this and says that he has come to see Sive. Mena lies, telling him that Sive is not at home. Liam doubts this as Sive's bike is outside. Mena insists that Sive is not there and tells Liam to leave. He politely refuses, saying he will wait for Sive. Mena becomes angrier and threatens to strike Liam with the fire tongs if he doesn't leave. Liam says that he loves Sive, but Mena scorns his claim and mocks him. There is a sharp contrast between Liam's composure and good manners and Mena's anger and rudeness.

> Liam says that he loves Sive, but Mena scorns his claim and mocks him

Mike enters and Mena quickly tells him that she did her best to get rid of Liam. Mike is calmer than his wife, but equally adamant that Liam shall not see Sive. Liam says that he heard from Pats Bocock and Carthalawn that Sive is getting married. Mike denies this but Liam asks him why Thomasheen Seán Rua and Seán Dóta are visiting the house every day if there is no truth in the story. He tells Mike that he has heard Seán Dóta talking to himself on the road, saying all the dirty things he will do to Sive once they are married. This touches a chord with Mike but he continues to deny that there is any match planned. Liam says that everyone in the village knows about the match and that 'the public-houses are full with the mockery of it'.

Mike becomes angry and threatens to hit Liam with his whip. Mena repeats her threat to take the tongs to him. Liam apologises for causing trouble and selflessly says that, if it will help, he will leave the area and not return until Sive is older. This effectively removes Mike's excuse for marrying Sive off quickly in order to prevent her continuing relationship with Liam. Liam goes on to beg Mike and Mena not to give Sive to 'that rotting old man with his gloating eyes and trembling hands'. He says that they will have to answer to God for their sins if they make such a match for money.

Mike knows that Liam is right, but he does not like to hear the truth. Mena is furious and grabs a knife, threatening to take it to Liam if he does not leave. Liam goes, but not before saying that Mena and Mike will regret their decision.

Sive enters looking a little pale and tired. She says she heard Liam's voice. Mena lies, telling Sive that he called to wish her the best in her married life and to say that he was leaving the area. Sive is astonished and very distressed to hear this. She cannot believe that Liam would abandon her. Crying, she goes back to her room.

Mike is unhappy because he knows Sive does not want to marry Seán Dóta, but Mena says that Sive is better off than she was when she married Mike. She reminds Mike that she had to cope with Nanna's constant insults and take on an orphaned baby. Mike remains unconvinced but Mena refuses to discuss the match any further. She leaves to get water and Mike begins to shave in preparation for calling to the priest to arrange the wedding.

Nanna enters and, like Liam, begs Mike not to allow the marriage to go ahead. She blames Mena for organising the match and says that she brought evil and bad luck to the house the day she married Mike. Mike is so uncomfortable about the match that he cannot meet Nanna's eye, but he claims that it is better for Sive to marry Seán Dóta than to

SUMMARY AND ANALYSIS

continue seeing Liam Scuab. He claims he is worried that Liam will get Sive pregnant the way Liam's cousin got her mother pregnant. Nanna says he should be ashamed of such thoughts. She insists that there is 'a sweet thing' in the love between Sive and Liam.

Mike becomes highly agitated as he tells Nanna that life is not perfect for anyone and that she has forgotten how Sive's mother met a sorry end because of love. He says that it is a good thing that Sive will be safely married while she is still young, innocent and pure. Nanna says that Mike is simply trying to justify the match and that Sive is 'for sale like an animal'. In a passionate temper, Mike gathers up his shaving things and storms off to the stable to shave in peace.

KEY QUESTIONS

- What is your impression of Liam Scuab?
- Do you think Nanna could do more to prevent Sive being sold 'like an animal'?
- What reasons does Mike give Nanna for agreeing to the match?
- Do you feel any sympathy for Mike when his wife and his mother each urge him to agree with them, or do you think he shows weakness in not coming to his own decision and standing by it?

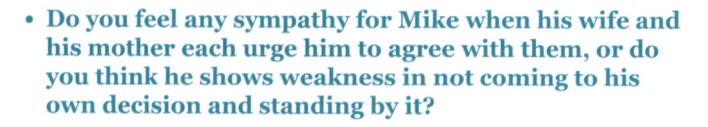

WRITING TASK

- Write the letter you think Sive might have written to Liam explaining how she feels about him and about the match.

❝ Important quotations

Liam to Mena and Mike, telling them that he has heard Seán Dóta talking to himself as he walks along the road

'Things about Sive, and how he will warm her before she is much older. A lot of other things too, but most of it not fit to mention'

Liam to Mena and Mike

'I promise I will leave these parts till Sive is a woman. I swear that on my dead mother. But do not give her to that rotting old man with the gloating eyes and trembling hands'

'With an oul' devil in the corner screechin' at me the length of the day and a dirty brat of an orphan bawling in the corner'	Mena to Mike, describing the early days of their marriage
'There was never an ounce of luck in this house since that greasy bitch darkened the door of it'	Nanna to Mike, referring to Mena
'There is a sweet thing in their love'	Nanna to Mike, referring to Sive and Liam
'Women must pay for all happiness. That is their sorry shape, God help us'	Nanna to Mike
'How can I go aisy when my own grandchild is for sale like an animal'	Nanna to Mike

Act 2, Scene 2

It is a fortnight later, the evening before the wedding. Nanna is alone in the kitchen when there is a knock at the door. It is Pats Bocock. He tells Nanna that he has been watching the house for hours for an opportunity to catch her alone. Nanna warns him that Mike is due home soon. Mena and Sive have gone to town for the day to buy clothes and drink for the wedding with the £50 Seán Dóta gave for the purpose.

Pats tells Nanna that Liam Scuab came to his caravan the night before and that he, Pats and Carthalawn have devised a plan to save Sive. When everyone has gone to bed, she must escape through the window and go to Liam's house. He will be waiting for her and they can get married first thing in the morning. Pats is impressed by the true love between Sive and Liam and he knows that Seán Dóta feels only lust for Sive, not love. He gives Nanna a letter from Liam to Sive and warns her not to let anyone see it. He says that he and Carthalawn will visit the house later to sing a song and give their blessing to the wedding. Pats believes this will allay any suspicion as it will appear that

SUMMARY AND ANALYSIS

they expect the marriage to take place.

Mike enters suddenly and is suspicious of Pats' motives for calling. He has seen him hanging around the house all day. Pats makes light of it, saying that he was planning to steal some eggs but thought better of it. Mike doesn't believe him and says that Pats knows he would always be welcome in the house and given food, so there is no reason not to come straight to the door rather than spying on them first. Pats denies that he was spying and politely takes his leave.

When Pats is gone, Mike asks Nanna what Pats was up to. Nanna says a son should not question his mother. Mike says that he has always tried to be a good son and a good husband. Nanna once again blames Mena for ruining the family's happiness and reminds Mike how much he used to love and care for Sive when she was little.

Mike is bothered by his mother's remarks and tells her that he cannot please both her and Mena at once. He says that he saw Nanna hiding something when he came in, and asks what it was. He suspects that she and Pats are up to something. Nanna shows him the letter but makes him promise not to tell anyone about it. She says that it is only Liam's farewell to Sive but that if Mena or Thomasheen were to find it they would burn it. Mike is still uneasy about Pats' involvement and asks Nanna if she is sure that is all the letter contains. Nanna assures him that it is and suggests that he give it to Sive himself. She says that she knows Mike is against the match and that by giving the letter to Sive he will be giving her some small measure of happiness; the last bit she will have until she dies. Mike is tormented with guilt and misery and agrees to give the letter to Sive, even though he feels bad about deceiving Mena. Nanna asks him not to read the letter, which makes Mike suspicious again. Nanna reassures him by saying that Sive would resent Mike reading a private message from Liam and points out that she didn't read it herself. She makes Mike promise to give it to Sive unopened. Mike agrees, but he is not happy about it.

Nanna leaves and Mike places the letter on the mantelpiece and stares at it for a while. Then he begins to sweep the kitchen. Thomasheen enters. He asks Mike if Mena and Sive are back from town yet. He knows that Seán Dóta gave Mena £50 to buy wedding clothes for Sive, but he suspects she will keep forty of those pounds for herself.

Mike takes the letter from the mantelpiece and tries to put it in his pocket without Thomasheen seeing. He does not succeed and Thomasheen gets it out of him that the letter is for Sive and was delivered by Pats Bocock. Thomasheen is alarmed and demands that Mike open it. Mike refuses, and Thomasheen mocks his stupidity in not realising that the letter might have something to do with the wedding. He snatches the letter from Mike and tears it open. He is illiterate so tells Mike to read it for him. Reluctantly, Mike reads Liam's letter aloud and both men learn that Liam is asking Sive to elope with him. Mike is moved by the sincerity of the sentiments expressed in the letter but Thomasheen is not. He mocks Liam's romantic language and says that he will never have a woman if he carries on like this. Thomasheen burns the letter, just as Nanna had predicted, and harshly tells Mike not to tell Sive about it. Mike is troubled and wonders aloud if he is 'doing right by the girl at all'. Thomasheen mocks him, saying he is as indecisive as an old hen.

> Thomasheen burns the letter, just as Nanna had predicted, and harshly tells Mike not to tell Sive about it

Mena and Sive return. Sive is wearing smart new clothes but appears dispirited and unhappy. She takes off one of her high-heeled shoes and rubs her foot. Mena is carrying parcels under her arms. She sends the men out to bring in the boxes of drink. They do so and then begin to help themselves to some of the porter. Mena tries to persuade Sive to eat or drink something, but Sive seems depressed and listless. Her discomfort and lethargy are in sharp contrast to the other characters present, who seem to be enjoying the party atmosphere of

SUMMARY AND ANALYSIS

the wedding preparations. Sive refuses food and drink, saying she has a headache and wants to go to bed. She leaves, walking slowly to her room.

Mena sends Mike out to untack the pony from the cart. When he is gone, she and Thomasheen talk about the wedding. Mena is anxious to get her hands on the money but Thomasheen says that Seán Dóta will give nothing until after the marriage ceremony. He tells Mena about the letter from Liam and about Mike's intention to give it to Sive. Mena calls Mike a fool but is relieved to hear that the letter is burnt. Thomasheen asks about Nanna, wondering if she is causing trouble, but Mena says she hasn't been out of her room for a few days. Thomasheen is pleased to hear this.

Mike returns and he and Thomasheen settle down to drink more of the porter. Mike says that Seán Dóta is on his way up the road and Thomasheen warns against giving him any alcohol lest he fall down and die on the way home, ruining their plans.

Seán Dóta enters. He has come to check that all the preparations for the wedding are in order. Mena reassures him and tells him that Sive is in her room, resting. Seán Dóta and Mike engage in small talk about the weather and farming. Mena busies herself preparing the evening meal. Mike offers Seán a drink but Mena quickly says that no man should have alcohol the night before his wedding. She offers Seán Dóta a lemonade instead, and lays a place for him at the table.

Mike alerts the others to the sound of a bodhrán outside. It is Pats Bocock and Carthalawn. They enter, singing a song blessing Sive and Seán Dóta's wedding. Mike welcomes them and offers them a drink. He asks them what news they have heard on their travels and Pats says that the country is changing. Farmers are making a lot of money now, he says, and they are rising up to become 'the new lords of the land'. He points at Seán Dóta as he says this, and says: 'God help the land!' Mena and Thomasheen flare up at this insult to Seán Dóta, and Thomasheen tells the tinkers to leave. Pats instructs Carthalawn to give Thomasheen his 'mighty best' and Carthalawn launches into a song cursing Thomasheen. Mike is delighted but Thomasheen and Mena are furious.

Seán Dóta gets up to leave but Mena urges him to stay, saying that Sive will want to see him before he goes. Seán Dóta is happy to wait if there is a chance of seeing Sive. Mena goes to get her. While they wait, Pats holds his hat out to Seán Dóta but the old man refuses to give him any money. Pats tells Seán Dóta that he is too old for Sive and that one squeeze from her will kill him. Seán Dóta is enraged but Pats is undaunted by the old man's anger. At his instruction, Carthalawn sings a song cursing Seán Dóta and saying that he will die soon.

At that moment, Mena rushes in, saying that Sive has gone. Thomasheen tells her to calm down and asks if Sive took any baggage. Mena replies that she took nothing, not even her shoes. Thomasheen hopes that Sive might be in Nanna's room, but a quick check shows that she is not.

Pats speaks up, saying that he thought he saw a girl running across the bog earlier but he didn't take any notice at the time. Now he thinks it might have been Sive. Mena is terrified that Sive might have fallen into a bog hole. She orders Mike to go and find her. Thomasheen says he will go with Mike and Seán Dóta volunteers to go too. Mena asks him to stay with her instead as she does not want to be alone.

Just then, a frantic voice is heard outside, calling for them to open the door and bring a light. It is Liam Scuab. He enters, carrying Sive's dead body in his arms. She is soaked through. Pats sweeps the ware off the table and Liam lays Sive's body on it. He folds her arms and calls for a cloth to dry her hair. Unnoticed by anyone, Thomasheen and Seán Dóta sneak towards the door and leave quietly.

> Unnoticed by anyone, Thomasheen and Seán Dóta sneak towards the door and leave quietly

Liam tells the others that he saw Sive running across the bog, 'letting cries out of her that would rend your heart'. He tried to stop her but she ran on and drowned herself in a bog hole. It was a while before Liam found her. He rounds on Mena, saying that it is her fault Sive took her own life. Mena is shocked and Liam yells at her to get away from Sive's body because her presence is 'polluting the pure

SUMMARY AND ANALYSIS

spirit of the child'. He raises his hand to strike her if she doesn't go. Mena runs to her room.

Liam begins to dry Sive's hair lovingly and carefully. Mike is terribly distressed and says he must go and fetch the priest. He begs Liam to go with him, grabbing the younger man as he speaks. Liam shakes off his grip violently but agrees to go with Mike as far as the main road. They leave.

Only Pats and Carthalawn remain with Sive's body. Carthalawn sings a sad, slow, tender song about Sive's death. He and Pats turn and leave, Carthalawn still singing as they go.

The lights in the kitchen fade and Nanna enters. She bows her head over her dead granddaughter and weeps silently. The singing outside dies away completely and there is silence.

KEY QUESTIONS

- Given the circumstances in which she found herself, do you think Sive had any option but to do something as extreme as taking her own life?

- 'Nanna is partly responsible for Sive's death.' Do you agree or disagree with this statement? Explain your answer with reference to the text.

- How do you think Sive's death will affect the relationships between Mike, Mena and Nanna?

WRITING TASK

- Write a piece about the play, *Sive*, beginning with one of the following statements:
  I enjoyed studying this play because …
  I did not enjoy studying this play because …

Important quotations

Nanna to Pats Bocock   'The poor child is nearly out of her mind these past weeks'

Pats to Nanna, referring to Seán Dóta's feelings for Sive   'He have no love for her. 'Tis the flesh of her he do be doting over'

'It is hard to be a good son and a good husband under the same roof'	Mike to Nanna
'Where is the love you used to have for Sive? ... Where is the promise you gave to your sister?'	Nanna to Mike
'A woman never knows from one minute to the next what way her mind is going to act ... You must make up their mind for them'	Thomasheen to Mike
'There was the quiet and the peace of what we felt for each other. I loved you then, Sive. I love you now ...'	Part of Liam's letter to Sive
'God direct me, but am I doing the right by the girl at all?'	Mike to Thomasheen
'There is money-making everywhere. The face of the country is changing'	Pats Bocock
'A squeeze out of a lively young girl would stop your heart, old man'	Pats to Seán Dóta
'I saw her running across the bog with only the little frock against the cold of the night. She ran like the wind and she letting cries out of her that would rend your heart'	Liam Scuab
'You killed her! ... You horrible filthy bitch!'	Liam to Mena
'You are polluting the pure spirit of the child with your nearness'	Liam to Mena
'Oh, they drowned lovely Sive, She would not be a bride, And they laid her for to bury in the clay'	Carthalawn

'The beautiful hair of her!
The lovely, silky white of her!'

Liam Scuab, act 2, scene 2

Noel O'Donovan (Seán Dóta), Ruth Bradley (Sive), Barry Ward (Liam Scaub), and Eamon Morrissey (Thomasheen Seán Rua) in Druid Theatre's 2003 production of Sive

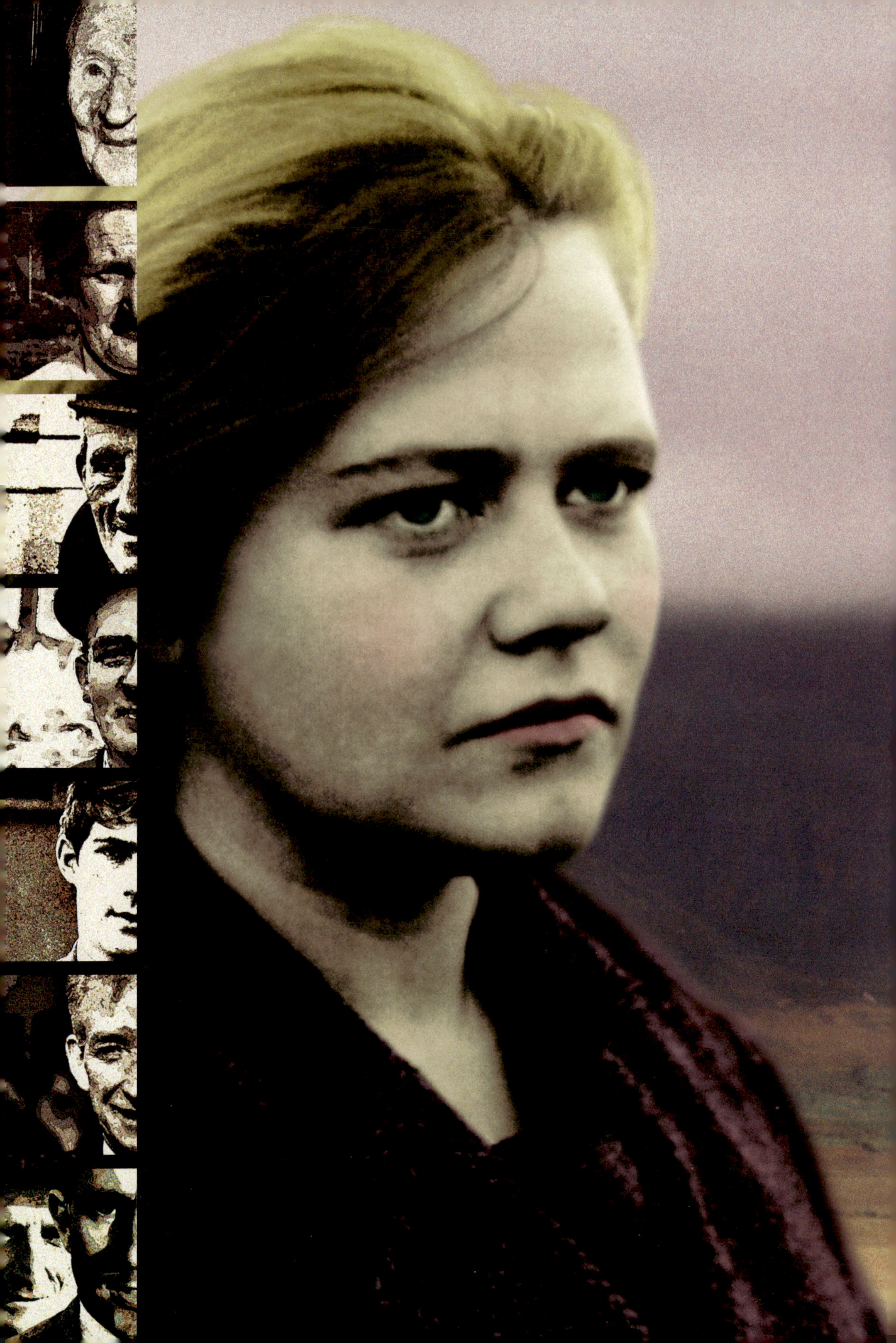

Character analysis 2

CHARACTER ANALYSIS

Sive Glavin

innocent
pure
refined
romantic
betrayed
tragic heroine

Innocent and pure

All of the descriptions of Sive highlight her innocence and youthful beauty. Liam Scuab says that Sive is known locally as 'the flower of the parish', and Mike compares her match with Seán Dóta to 'tossing the white flower of the canavaun on to the manure heap'. When he is pleading with Mike and Mena to reconsider the match, Liam compares Sive to Christ in that she is a pure, virtuous soul being offered up for sacrifice by sinful people: 'Will ye stand and watch each other draw the hard, crooked thorns deep into His helpless body?'

Refined

Sive is well educated and intelligent. When we first meet her, she is carrying a satchel of books and seems to be a diligent student. Her refinement and education are in sharp contrast to the coarseness of other characters. Only Liam Scuab is a suitable match for her. When Seán Dóta recites a foolish, childish rhyme in an effort to impress Sive, we see how inappropriate it is that she should ever be linked with such a man.

Romantic

Mike says of Sive that 'she will be dreaming about love with a young man', and he is correct in this. Sive and Liam Scuab's relationship is untainted by any of the baser sentiments expressed by the other characters. They do not speak of lust or of the need for dowries, but instead relish the simplicity of time spent together. In his letter to Sive, Liam describes 'the quiet and the peace' of the starry nights they spent together when Sive could get away from her family.

The idea of matchmaking is abhorrent to Sive. She speaks incredulously of 'two people who never saw each other before' getting married, and tells Liam that it is horrible and that she could never do such a thing.

Sive's romantic nature and her love for Liam mean that she cannot possibly contemplate marrying Seán Dóta, no matter how wealthy he is. She cannot understand or agree with Mena's urging that she should dwell on the 'handling of thousands and the fine clothes and perfumery'.

Betrayed

Sive has no parents and must rely on Mike to act as a father figure to her. He has a great affection for his niece and Nanna reminds him that when she was younger he used to take her everywhere with him: 'You were better than a father to her.' When the match is proposed, however, Mike betrays Sive. He sides with Mena and Thomasheen, even though he is unhappy about it.

Mike disapproves of Liam Scuab, which is part of the reason he is willing to allow Seán Dóta to buy the girl in marriage. He betrays Sive twice over the issue of Liam. The first time is when Mena tells Sive that Liam visited briefly, not to see her particularly but to wish her well in her marriage and tell her that he is emigrating. Mike sees Sive's distress when she hears this lie but he does nothing to correct the impression.

The second time Sive is betrayed by her uncle is when Mike reads Liam's letter aloud but keeps the contents to himself after it is burned by Thomasheen. Although he could no longer give the letter itself to Sive, Mike could have told her that Liam loved her still and that he wanted to marry her. That he didn't do so is a dreadful betrayal of his niece's trust. After all, up to this point his argument against the relationship was that he believed Liam's intentions were not honourable. Now he knows the young man intends to marry Sive immediately, but still he keeps this information from her.

CHARACTER ANALYSIS: **SIVE GLAVIN**

The result of these lies is that Sive believes it is Liam who has betrayed her, and she is so distraught and grief-stricken that she sees no option other than to take her own life.

Tragic heroine

Sive is a symbol of virtue and innocence in the play and for this reason she is not perhaps as fully developed a character as some of the others. Certainly, it could be argued that it is unrealistic to have a character so perfectly virtuous and innocent, but Sive's perfection highlights the evildoing of those who plot to marry her off against her will. Because she is without fault, the behaviour of Mena, Mike and Thomasheen is seen clearly as being despicable. Sive can in no way be held to account for any of the trouble that befalls her. She is a victim of those who seek to exploit her for their own purposes. They are stronger and more determined than she is, and use her docile, trusting nature to manipulate her and crush her spirit. She is reminiscent of other tragic heroines such as Juliet and Ophelia. Like Juliet, she is gradually isolated from those she might have expected to love and support her, and like Ophelia she is cynically used by others who see her only as a means to serve their own interests. Sive's decision to take her own life rather than enter into a loveless marriage is very much in keeping with the tradition of tragic heroines in literature. Her death is the death of virtue, innocence and love, and is deeply shocking for the audience and the other characters in the play.

Nanna Glavin

Loving grandmother

Nanna adores her granddaughter. In the absence of Sive's mother and in the face of Mena's open hatred of the girl, Nanna lavishes love and attention on her. Mena resents their closeness and accuses Sive of spending her time 'cohackling with that oul' boody woman in the corner'.

Nanna is Sive's confidante and the only person in the house to whom she can admit her deepest feelings, such as her love for Liam. Nanna conspires to help the pair meet, even though she knows Mike disapproves of Liam and would put a stop to the relationship were he to learn of it. It is to Nanna that Sive turns when Seán Dóta makes an aggressive pass at her on the road. She expresses her fear that some sort of plan is being hatched to set her up with Seán Dóta, and Nanna takes her concern seriously.

The love between Nanna and Sive is a source of comfort and support to the young girl. They share a room, and Nanna fusses over Sive, fetching her drinks of milk while she studies and so forth. This does not go unnoticed by Mena, who tells Thomasheen that Nanna has 'the charming of the girl in her hands. They are as thick as thieves, the pair of them.' Consequently, her first move when she wants to break Sive's spirit and get her to agree to the match is to announce that she can no longer sleep in the same room as Nanna.

Courageous

Nanna has no real power or authority in the house (something Mena is quick to remind her of whenever the chance arises) but still she tries her best to prevent Sive being forced to marry Seán Dóta. She begs

loving grandmother
courageous
hurtful
powerless
vulnerable
naive
heartbroken
alone

CHARACTER ANALYSIS: NANNA GLAVIN

Mike not to allow it to go ahead, and stands up for Liam Scuab when Mike claims that he wants to take advantage of Sive: 'There is a sweet thing in their love. Shame to you, Mike!'

The greatest courage Nanna shows is in dealing with Mena and Thomasheen. She tells them that the match is 'the devil's work' and that there is 'a hatchery of sin' in the house since they began their plotting. Both Mena and Thomasheen round on the vulnerable old woman, threatening her with the county home and destitution. Mena even goes so far as to open the door and invite Nanna to 'go on and put your bag on your back and go begging from door to door'. Although Nanna knows that she cannot defeat the pair, she holds her ground. Perhaps imprudently, she once again provokes Mena by commenting on her childlessness. Mena makes to strike her but is held back by Thomasheen. Nanna takes her leave, but as she does so she bravely repeats her assertion that the proposed match is evil and sinful.

> *'There is a sweet thing in their love. Shame to you, Mike!'*

Hurtful

Nanna has a hot temper and can be extremely cruel when she talks to Mena. There is no doubt that Mena provokes Nanna, but Nanna gives as good as she gets. She scorns Mena's poor background, claiming that her family drank tea 'out of jam pots for the want of cups', and calling Mena's father 'a half-starved bocock of a beggar'.

Most hurtful, however, are Nanna's frequent jibes about Mena's childlessness. This is the one topic which is sure to wound and enrage Mena, and Nanna does not hesitate to use this most powerful weapon in her verbal arsenal. She jeers that Mena is 'as dry as the hobs of hell inside', and tells her that all the local women of her age have children, while there is 'nothing to show by you'.

The ability to wound Mena with these jibes is the only power Nanna has over her bullying daughter-in-law. While it is at best unwise and at worst unkind of her to goad Mena with her infertility, it is the only way she can fight back when being attacked. For example, when Mena and Thomasheen pair up to insult and abuse her, Nanna manages to seize a passing reference to children in the cradle and repeat it in such a way as to provoke Mena into completely losing her temper. Although it is a cruel taunt, it must be remembered that shortly before Nanna made this remark she had been jeered at for being old and alone, had been told that her son didn't care about her, and that she was lucky not to be thrown out to wander the roads as a beggar or end up in the county home. The need to defend herself against such vicious abuse may explain, if not excuse, Nanna's cruel comments.

Nanna has not a kind word to say about Mena at any stage in the play. She tells Sive not to listen to Mena's 'poison prattle', claiming that it is simply a 'disease in her system'. Later in the play, when it seems inevitable that the match will go ahead, Nanna criticises Mena to Mike, calling her a 'greasy bitch', a 'hungry sow' and a 'pauperised wretch'.

Vulnerable and powerless

Nanna's vulnerability is obvious from the outset. The stage directions tell us that she is 'idly' tending the fire while 'surreptitiously smoking a clay pipe', which she hastily hides when she hears the door opening. The impression we get is of a woman who has nothing to do and who is tense and ill at ease in her own home.

At the time the play was written, it was not uncommon for three generations of the same family to live under one roof. The mother-in-law was meant to hand over the running of the house to her new daughter-in-law. The older woman would then assist in rearing the children and would be looked after and treated with respect by the younger family members. Although this could work well on occasion, it often led to great tension, as is the case in *Sive*. Nanna refuses to acknowledge Mena's authority in the house, while Mena tells Nanna that she is a burden and should have been put in her place long ago.

The result of this tension is that Nanna is in a vulnerable and powerless position in the house. Mena has no children for her to rear and there is nothing for Nanna to do. Mena has no respect for her, and Mike dances to Mena's tune, telling his mother that 'a horse can't be

CHARACTER ANALYSIS: **NANNA GLAVIN**

guided by two roads at once'.

Nanna's powerlessness and vulnerability are brought sharply to the fore in the third scene of Act 1. She is alone with Mena and Thomasheen and they seize an opportunity to attack her for objecting to the match. They tell Nanna that she is very foolish to fight with them when she has no one to back her up. They point out that her husband is dead and that her son doesn't care about her. She is threatened with the county home and destitution, and scorned for her dependence on Mike and Mena.

> She is threatened with the county home and destitution, and scorned for her dependence on Mike and Mena

Nanna has no power to stop the match. She appeals to Mike, but even her hold over him has largely vanished since he married Mena. Nanna reminds him that she is his mother and that she has loved him 'as no one ever will'. Mike, though he feels uncomfortable about the match, sides with Mena and refuses to be swayed by Nanna's pleas.

Naive

Perhaps it is because Mike is her son, and she loves him despite his faults, that Nanna makes a grave error of judgement in Act 2. Pats has entrusted her with a letter from Liam to Sive, but when Mike spots it and asks what it is, Nanna tells him. Not only that, but she goes so far as to give him the letter and to ask him to pass it on to Sive himself. Nanna is not completely honest with Mike about the contents of the letter, insisting that it is only Liam 'saying goodbye to [Sive] in his own way'.

Heartbroken and alone

Nanna's distress at the end of the play is deeply moving. She emerges from her room when Pats and Carthalawn have left and weeps silently over the body of her beloved Sive. She is alone with the dead girl and we are struck by the fact that Nanna has nobody left to love or to love her. Her husband, daughter and now her granddaughter are dead. Her relationship with her son is unlikely ever to recover from Sive's death and the role Mike played in it. Nanna has lost everything and we cannot help but mourn with her.

Mena Glavin

Insecure

Mena is in a strange position in the Glavin household. Strictly speaking, Nanna should have relinquished her authority in the family home once Mike married, but she is unwilling to do so. She refers to the house as hers and scorns Mena for not having children and for coming from a very poor background. Mena asserts that she has 'every right to this house', but Nanna snaps back: 'I was here before you.'

Bitter and resentful

Mena is an unhappy woman, filled with bitterness about her life. She married Mike to get away from the poverty of her family home, but wishes now that she had waited a bit longer and found a better match for herself. She has no children and blames Mike for that, asking Nanna, 'Is it my fault that your son is a tired gomeril of a man?'

Mena deeply resents having to put up with Nanna and Sive. She tells Mike that when she married him she had to cope with 'an oul' devil in the corner screechin' at me the length of the day and a dirty brat of an orphan bawling in the corner'. Sive's continued education is another bone of contention in the Glavin household. Mena had no such opportunity herself and does not see why she and Mike should have to work hard to provide for Sive when she is old enough to make her own living: 'Why should that young rip be sent to a convent every day instead of being out earning with a farmer?'

Mike and Nanna's preferential treatment of Sive contributes to Mena's resentment of the girl. She accuses Sive of 'cohackling with that oul' boody woman in the corner' and suspects the pair of conspiring against her. Mena even begrudges Sive small things such

insecure
bitter
resentful
unromantic
mercenary
manipulative
bullying

CHARACTER ANALYSIS: **MENA GLAVIN**

as the cup of creamy milk Nanna fetches her: 'The top of the tank for her ladyship!'

Mike's affection for Sive angers Mena. He objects to the match between his niece and Seán Dóta on the grounds that Sive is too young and too romantic to be married off for the sake of money. Mena asks him indignantly, 'And wasn't I young?' Mena feels bitter about the fact that Sive has chances in life that she never had. Even the match with Seán Dóta promises to make Sive far wealthier than Mena could ever hope to be: 'Twenty cows and money to burn! She'll do no better for all her airs and graces. Look at the match I made … four cows on the side of a mountain and a few acres of bog.'

> Mena feels bitter about the fact that Sive has chances in life that she never had

Unromantic

Mena did not marry for love, but to get away from the poverty of her family home. She tells Sive that she had to share a small room with her sisters: 'There was no corner of the bed we could call our own.' Mena scrimped and saved to make enough money to bring to her marriage, but tells Nanna that she wishes now she had waited a little longer and made a better match for herself than a 'poor amadawn' who worked in the bog.

Thomasheen shrewdly guesses that there is no romance or real love in Mike and Mena's marriage. He says that Mike 'would sooner to stick his snout in a plate of mate and cabbage, or to rub the back of a fattening pig than whisper a bit of his fondness for you'.

Mena's own experience of marriage leads her to believe that it is something people become accustomed to rather than go into willingly with open eyes and a glad heart. When Mike says that Sive has 'no heart' for the match, Mena asks him indignantly, 'What way was I when I came to this house? No one to say a good word for me and amn't I coming into my own now in spite of it all?'

Mena's lack of romantic sentiment means that she has no understanding of or empathy with Sive's feelings and her desire to marry for love. Mena would leap at the chance to marry a man as wealthy as Seán Dóta. When Sive protests that she could 'never live with that old man', Mena reminds her of his wealth and asks Sive to think of how much better off she will be than most of the other women in the parish.

Mercenary

Money is everything to Mena. She grew up in an impoverished household where she and her sisters had 'no corner of a bed we could call our own'. She tells Sive: 'We used to sit into the night talking and thieving and wondering where the next ha'penny would come from.' Money was the only means of escape from such misery. Mena made enough to allow her to marry Mike but she lives in constant fear of being poor. She grudges every penny that is spent on Sive's education and when Mike makes money at the market she tells him that they will 'mind whatever penny we make'.

Mena's love of money and her belief that marriage is simply a business transaction by which people may better themselves means that, as soon as she hears the full details of the match, Sive's fate is sealed. Thomasheen has judged well and is aware that the lure of £200 and the promise of being rid of Sive and Nanna will win Mena over to the idea of selling Sive to a lecherous old farmer: 'I knew my woman from the start.'

Sive's objection to the marriage is incomprehensible to Mena. While she sees that Seán Dóta is a very unattractive man, she honestly believes that his wealth should be enough to persuade Sive to overlook his other faults.

> *'We used to sit into the night talking and thieving and wondering where the next ha'penny would come from'*

Manipulative

When Thomasheen enlists Mena's help in arranging the match, he makes a wise choice. Although it is a difficult task, Mena manipulates those around her to achieve her ends.

CHARACTER ANALYSIS: **MENA GLAVIN**

Mike is her first challenge. He objects vehemently to the match, but Mena begins to win him around by telling him that 'there is a gift of £200 for us'. She reminds him of Sive's illegitimacy and says they are lucky that anyone will marry the girl 'with the slur and the doubt hanging over her'. Taking Thomasheen's advice, she uses her sexuality to tempt Mike, telling him that with Sive and Nanna gone, they will have the house to themselves. When that fails, Mena mocks Mike's manhood, calling him a 'man of straw'.

Mena eventually wins Mike around to her way of thinking, even though he still has doubts. Next, Mena has to persuade Sive to marry a man she detests. Mena's methods are diabolical but clever. She breaks Sive down by telling her that she is 'a common bye-child – a bastard'; isolates her from Nanna's support by moving her to a bedroom beside her own; prevents her from going to school any more; and, in an act of dreadful cruelty, she tells Sive that Liam wishes her well in her married life and that he is emigrating for good.

Bullying

Mena relentlessly bullies those around her and will not allow anyone to stand in the way of her earning £200 from the match. Anyone who does oppose her is instantly and viciously attacked. Mike is mocked as a 'man of straw' for objecting to the marriage, and when he leaves the kitchen in a rage at being so insulted, Mena refuses to give in and follows him out the door.

Nanna is bullied and threatened dreadfully when she tells Mena and Thomasheen that the match is 'the devil's work' and that there is 'a hatchery of sin' in the house. Mena threatens to throw Nanna out of the house and make her beg for a living, and even moves to strike the old woman but is held back by Thomasheen.

Mena also intimidates Sive and does all she can to break the girl's spirit. Not content with brutally revealing Sive's illegitimacy to her, she drives away Liam Scuab and lies to Sive about his visit, saying that he called to wish her happiness in her married life and to say that he was 'going away altogether to foreign places'.

Thomasheen Seán Rua

Cunning and manipulative

Thomasheen Seán Rua is an untrustworthy man and a master of manipulation and cunning. The stage directions tells us that he is 'shifty-looking, ever on his guard'. He ensures that he has Mena alone before broaching the topic of the match, as he rightly judges that she is the only one in the family who would entertain the suggestion. He also knows that she will do almost anything for money, and that she is forceful enough to make Mike and Sive do what she wants. His final, crafty stroke of genius is telling Mena that Seán Dóta will have Nanna to live with Sive.

As well as getting Mena to agree to the match, Thomasheen suggests ways in which she might win Mike and Sive round. He advises Mena to use her sexual wiles on Mike and tells her to intimidate and bully Sive into the match by threatening to reveal the story of her illegitimacy. Mena is doubtful that this approach will work, so Thomasheen says that she could try to entice Sive with the promise of money and an old husband who will die soon, leaving her a rich widow. In the event, it is Thomasheen's first suggestion that contributes to breaking Sive's spirit when she shows no interest whatsoever in marrying for money.

When Mike says that the match is a bad idea and that Sive is too romantic to consent to such a thing, Thomasheen cunningly tells him that Sive has been secretly meeting Liam Scuab. He knows this will anger Mike and that he will want to do something to put a stop to it. He is right, and Mike finally agrees that it is better for Sive to marry Seán Dóta than to end up like her mother.

cunning
manipulative
unromantic
misogynistic
pathetic
dishonourable
cowardly
amoral

> Thomasheen tells Mena to intimidate and bully Sive into the match by threatening to reveal the story of her illegitimacy

CHARACTER ANALYSIS: **THOMASHEEN SEÁN RUA**

Unromantic/misogynistic

Although Thomasheen's job is bringing people together in marriage, he has a very poor opinion of relationships and of women. He compares Sive to a pony being bought at auction, telling Mena that he will 'not rest happy until [Seán Dóta] has the halter on her'. He tells Mike that a woman is as unpredictable and indecisive as 'a giddy heifer on the road to the fair'. When Mike reads out Liam's letter to Sive, Thomasheen is scornful of the romantic sentiments expressed in it. He thinks Liam is foolish to woo Sive in this manner and is bewildered by Liam's apology for 'beginning to wax poetic': 'He will never have a woman the way he is going about it! There is no wax in the ketching of women. There is the ketchin' of a hoult until she is winded. That's the time for words with a woman.'

Pathetic

Part of the reason for Thomasheen's attitude to women and relationships is his loneliness and his inability to find love in his own life. He admits to Mena that it is difficult to be a single man: 'I know what it is to be alone in a house when the only word you will hear is a sigh, the sigh of a fire in the hearth dying, with no human words to warm you.'

> *'Love! In the name of God, what do the likes of us know about love?'*

Thomasheen did love a girl once and had saved up almost enough to marry her when his father committed suicide and Thomasheen had to spend all his money on the funeral. This may be part of the reason for his pragmatic and mercenary attitude to love and marriage now. Like Mena, he views it as a business arrangement, and when Mike says that Sive does not love Seán Dóta, Thomasheen says incredulously, 'Love! In the name of God, what do the likes of us know about love?'

Dishonourable, amoral and cowardly

Thomasheen, like Mena, will let nothing stand in the way of the marriage. He is determined to get his share of the matchmaking fee and does not care whose life or happiness he destroys in order to achieve his aim. He is well aware that Sive loves Liam Scuab and that Seán Dóta's only interest in Sive is a lustful one.

Nanna despises Thomasheen, saying, 'The mean snap is in you and all that went before you.' Thomasheen knows Nanna opposes him, so he bullies and intimidates her every chance he gets. He does not do so in front of Mike, but waits until he and Mena have Nanna alone and vulnerable.

At the end of the play, when Liam carries Sive's body into the house, Thomasheen takes a quick look at the dead girl, then 'edges slyly away and exits looking around him furtively'. He realises the role he has played in Sive's death but has not the moral courage to face up to it. He exits the play in the same sneaky and underhand way that he first entered, as dishonourable and self-serving as ever.

CHARACTER ANALYSIS

Mike Glavin

hardworking
mercenary
weak
emasculated
naive
gentle
loving
torn

Hardworking

Mike Glavin works hard to provide for his family. He has to support his wife, mother and niece, and he appears to do so to the best of his ability. Sive's mother wanted him to educate the girl, and even though it is expensive, Mike does so. He is rarely at rest in the play; even when he is sitting by the fire he is mending an old horse harness.

Life on a remote hill farm with only a few cows and not much land is difficult. Mike has to do all he can to keep his family fed and clothed, and he has seen hard times. He tells Mena that it is good to see things improving and that 'it makes a change from beggin' and pinchin' with our craws often only half-filled'.

Mercenary

Money is very important to Mike, probably because he has often been without it. When he comes home from the market, having done well in the sale of animals, he tells Mena, 'Money is the best friend a man ever had.' Mena knows this is Mike's weakness and that it is the way she will be able to come around him about the match: 'He has a great love for the few pounds.'

Mike does not approve of the match between Sive and Seán Dóta. He initially refuses to countenance it, but is browbeaten and manipulated into agreeing by Mena and Thomasheen. He is not happy about the proposed marriage as he knows that Sive is miserable, but he admits that 'the money is a great temptation'.

Weak and emasculated

Although Mike is the man of the house, he is no match for Mena. She is a far stronger character than he is, and she has no respect for him. She scorns him to Nanna, calling him a 'poor amadawn' and a 'half-fool', and she attacks his masculinity when he refuses to listen to her about the match: 'Go away, man of straw!' When Nanna taunts Mena with her childlessness, Mena replies that it is not her fault but Mike's, calling him 'a tired gomeril of a man'.

Mena is not the only one who views Mike as weak. Thomasheen does not show him anything like the respect he shows Mena, speaking insultingly to him and ordering him around in his own house. He calls to the house one evening and, on catching Mike sweeping the kitchen floor, says mockingly that he would have made a great housekeeper. When Mike says that he intends to give Liam's letter to Sive, Thomasheen is exasperated: 'It comes to me that you are the greatest lump of a fool, of an eejit, of a dul amú, in the seven parishes. You shouldn't be trusted with a quenched match.' Mike allows Thomasheen to force him to read the letter aloud, even though he thinks it is the wrong thing to do. Thomasheen burns the letter when Mike has finished, pushing Mike away when he tries to stop him and overruling Mike's objections with insults: 'Will you hold your tongue, you bleddy oinseach! Keep your gob shut.'

> Thomasheen does not show him anything like the respect he shows Mena, speaking insultingly to him and ordering him around in his own house

Mike allows himself to be bullied into agreeing to a match he knows in his heart is wrong because he does not have the strength to stand up to his forceful, aggressive wife or the conniving Thomasheen.

Naive

Mike does not seem to realise how he is being manipulated by Mike and Mena. Mena uses his love of money to persuade him to agree to the match, while Thomasheen plays on his fear that Liam Scuab may take advantage of Sive: 'I don't want her going the same road as her mother.'

It never occurs to Mike to plot and plan the way the other characters

CHARACTER ANALYSIS: **MIKE GLAVIN**

do. He believes Nanna when she assures him that the letter she has been asked to deliver to Sive has 'no harm in it' and is just Liam 'saying good-bye to her in his own way'. Just as manipulated by Nanna as he was by Mena and Thomasheen, Mike agrees to give the letter to Sive. His suspicions about its contents have been allayed by Nanna's false assurances that the letter contains nothing detrimental to the match.

Gentle and loving

Mike has no romance or real love in his own marriage, but that does not mean that he does not recognise its importance to others. He is vehemently opposed to the match between Sive and Seán Dóta when he hears of it first, saying it would be 'like tossing the white flower of the canavaun on to the manure heap'. He knows Sive has a romantic soul and that 'she will be dreaming about love with a young man'. He has adored his niece since she was a baby, and Nanna plays on this when pleading with him not to allow the match to go ahead: 'Where is the love you used to have for Sive? Everywhere you went you used to take her with you. You were better than a father to her.'

Torn

Mike is in a difficult position. He genuinely wants to do his best by the three women he lives with, but that is next to impossible because of the hostility that exists between them: 'It is hard to be a good son and a good husband under the same roof.' To please Mena, Mike must agree to the match. However, by so doing he distresses Nanna and Sive. On top of this, Mike's own conscience tells him that what he is doing is wrong: 'God direct me, but am I doing right by the girl at all?'

'God direct me, but am I doing right by the girl at all?'

Mike is haunted by the memory of Sive's mother, his sister, who died after giving birth to the girl out of wedlock. He is determined that Sive will not end up the same way, and is deeply suspicious of Liam Scuab because it was Liam's cousin who got Sive's mother pregnant. Although Liam claims that his cousin intended to marry Sive's mother but died before he could set up a home for her in England, Mike does not appear to believe this, scorning Liam's story: 'You bring your tale well, don't you? Quick words and book-readin' like all belonging to you. Like your bloody cousin.'

In trying to do the right thing by everyone, Mike pleases no one. Mena despises him for his indecisiveness and his concern for Sive's happiness, Nanna is appalled that he allows the match to go ahead, and Sive is heartbroken to be separated from Liam and forced to accept Seán Dóta instead. Although there was no choice Mike could have made that would have pleased all three women in his life, the decision he makes in the end leads to the worst possible consequence. The death of Sive will undoubtedly haunt Mike for the rest of his life.

CHARACTER ANALYSIS

Liam Scuab

attractive
honourable
refined
eloquent
loving
loyal

A perfect match for Sive

The stage directions tell us that Liam is 'good-looking and manly, his voice cultured and refined'. Everything about him is the antithesis (complete opposite) of Seán Dóta. Liam is an ideal match for Sive and he loves her dearly. Like Sive, Liam is intelligent and better educated than the rest of the characters. They speak in the same way, using little or none of the vernacular or coarse talk that marks the language of the other characters.

Liam and Sive have a perfect relationship. They never argue, and seem to see eye to eye on everything. Liam is as horrified as Sive at the thought of matchmaking: 'Imagine making a marriage between two people who never saw each other before.'

Honourable and decent

Mike suspects Liam of wanting to take advantage of Sive, but nothing could be further from the truth. Nanna assures Mike that he would make a good husband for Sive and tells him: 'There is a sweet thing in their love.' Liam is open about his intentions from the start. When Mike says that Liam is only after Sive for one thing, Liam does not rise to the insult but says calmly, 'I say that I am after Sive and nothing more than that. I love her.'

> *'I say that I am after Sive and nothing more than that. I love her.'*

In a selfless gesture which shows just how honourable his intentions are, Liam offers to leave the area if that will persuade Mike that he is no threat and that there is no need to marry Sive off to 'that rotting old man with his gloating eyes and trembling hands'. This offer is ignored, but Mena later twists Liam's words in a diabolical way, telling Sive that Liam is 'going away altogether to foreign places'.

Eloquent and refined

Mike and Thomasheen scorn Liam's way of expressing himself. Mike accuses him of having 'quick words and book-readin' like all belonging to you', while Thomasheen says that he uses 'fine words' to win Sive.

Although he is insulted, mocked and abused by Mike and Mena, Liam never lowers himself to their level. When he pleads with them not to allow Sive to marry Seán Dóta, Mike and Mena threaten him with physical violence, Mike saying that he will 'take the whip' to him, and Mena saying that she will use the tongs from the fire to burn 'streaks on you worse than a raddle stick'. Liam responds politely and calmly, saying, 'I tell you I want no trouble. If I have upset ye, I'm sorry.'

> Liam's behaviour is in stark contrast to that of Seán Dóta, who makes an aggressive pass at Sive the first time he is alone with her

Antithesis of Seán Dóta

Liam treats Sive with love and respect, unlike Seán Dóta. In his letter to Sive, he recalls: '... the nights, the starry nights, we spent together in the bog. There was the quiet and the peace of what we felt for each other.' Liam's behaviour is in stark contrast to that of Seán Dóta, who makes an aggressive pass at Sive the first time he is alone with her. Pats Bocock describes Liam as 'a fine gradhbhar boy' who has 'a true heart' for Sive, and he tells Nanna that Seán Dóta 'have no love for her ... only the flesh of her he do be doting over'.

Deeply loving and loyal

Early in the play, Liam tells Sive: 'I would marry nobody but you, Sive. I love you.' They arrange to meet secretly and Liam vows to 'wait till the crack of dawn' for Sive, despite her request that he go home if she doesn't manage to sneak out of the house at the arranged time. Liam is loyal to Sive until the end, doing all he can to help her. When he is

CHARACTER ANALYSIS: LIAM SCUAB

forbidden from seeing Sive, he collaborates with Pats Bocock and Carthalawn in a plan to spirit Sive away to the city and marry her immediately. Tragically, Sive never learns of the plan and takes her own life in despair. It is Liam who sees her in her final moments and tries in vain to catch up with her as she runs across the bog.

Liam, who in a few hours' time should have been carrying Sive over the threshold as a young bride, instead carries her dead body into the Glavins' house. His love for Sive and his anguish at her death are heartbreakingly clear. He curses Mena, calling her a 'horrible filthy bitch' who 'hunted the poor little girl to her grave'. He cannot bear to have Mena near Sive, even in death, saying that she is 'polluting the pure spirit of the child'. Lovingly and gently, he dries Sive's hair with a cloth: 'The beautiful hair of her! The lovely, silky white of her!'

> *'The beautiful hair of her! The lovely, silky white of her!'*

Seán Dóta

Unappealing

unappealing
lecherous
ungenerous
mean-spirited

Seán Dóta's primary function in the play is to represent everything that a young girl like Sive would find unattractive, and to be the antithesis of Liam Scuab. He is a one-dimensional character who does not develop as the play progresses.

The stage directions tell us that Seán Dóta is a 'small man, a little wizened'. He is at least thirty-seven, and possibly as much as fifty years older than Sive. Mike describes him as 'a worn, exhausted little lurgadawn of a man'.

Everything about this elderly farmer is repulsive, even his mannerisms. Seán Dóta has an irritating habit of giving a little half-laugh whenever he speaks, and what he has to say is not of any interest to Sive. She is educated and refined, while he believes that poets are 'filled with roguery and they have the bad tongue on top of it, the thieves'. The poem he recites in an effort to impress Sive is dreadful. It is a childish, nonsensical rhyme with no merit whatsoever. Even the subject matter, hanging a child for stealing food from its mother and burying the body in dung, is deeply unpleasant. That Seán Dóta could think such a thing would please a girl like Sive shows how unsuitable he is for her. We cannot help but contrast this with the beautiful letter Liam sends Sive, in which he waxes lyrical about the starry nights they spent together.

'filled with roguery and they have the bad tongue on top of it, the thieves'

Lecherous

Thomasheen makes no secret of the fact that the only reason Seán Dóta

CHARACTER ANALYSIS: SEÁN DÓTA

wants to marry Sive is that he lusts after her. He has seen her cycling to the convent school every day, and Thomasheen says that he is obsessed with the girl to the point where he will do anything to have her. Pats observes to Nanna that Seán Dóta has 'no love for Sive. 'Tis the flesh of her he do be doting over.' Liam tells Mike and Mena that he has heard Seán Dóta talking to himself on the road, saying 'things about Sive and how he will warm her before she is much older. A lot of other things, too, but most if it not fit to mention again.'

When Seán Dóta does manage to get Sive on his own on the walk down the bohareen, he makes an aggressive pass at her. Sive is disgusted and appalled, telling Nanna that 'he nearly tore the coat off me' and saying that she only escaped by running into the neighbour's house.

Ungenerous and mean-spirited

He may be wealthy, but Seán Dóta is not a generous man. He does offer to pay quite a lot of money for Sive, but Thomasheen tells Mena that he will not part with 'a farthing of it' until the marriage goes ahead. He refuses to give any money to Pats and Carthalawn, scorning Pats' request with a sharp: 'How soft you have it! Money for nothing, how are you?'

When Liam carries Sive's body into the house at the end of the play, Seán Dóta says nothing but sneaks out of the house with Thomasheen. There is no hint that he feels any sorrow over Sive's death, but his furtive way of leaving suggests that he does realise that he is partly responsible for what happened.

Pats Bocock and Carthalawn

Travelling commentators

Pats and Carthalawn travel the roads in their caravan, stopping off to perform songs and bring news to people living in remote areas. In return for this, they usually receive gifts of food or money.

The tinkers are set apart from the other characters by their rather exotic costumes and by the way they express their opinions through curses and songs. The stage directions that introduce them go into some detail about their appearance and manner. Both wear shabby dress suits, incongruously matched with strong boots. Pats carries a stick and Carthalawn a bodhrán.

The father and son are not really individual characters, but function together as a sort of small Greek chorus, commenting on the unfolding events, the themes in the play and reflecting the playwright's attitude to the characters. They march in step with one another, which the playwright says shows that they 'have an understanding between each other'.

Pats and Carthalawn bring with them the news of the day and, in so doing, give the audience background information which helps them understand the world in which the play is set. Pats tells the characters assembled in the Glavins' kitchen on the night before the wedding that 'the face of the country is changing', and that the social order is being subverted. The poor are becoming rich and people like Seán Dóta will be the new 'lords of the land'. The playwright's attitude to this change is shown when Pats follows this remark with 'God help the land!'

travellers
commentators
Greek chorus
bygone era
decent
honourable

> Pats and Carthalawn bring with them the news of the day and, in so doing, give the audience background information

CHARACTER ANALYSIS: **PATS BOCOCK** AND **CARTHALAWN**

Represent a bygone era

Poets were traditionally believed to possess great, almost mystical, power in Ireland. There was a tradition of such men wandering the roads, delivering satirical, praising or cursing verses, depending on the reception they received. People feared and respected them because of the power of their language and their knowledge of the wider world. However, the power of the travelling poets is diminishing in the world of *Sive*. Nanna adheres to the old ways, saying that Pats and Carthalawn are 'people of the road – travelling people. They are above the class beggar'; but Mena denies them food or money. Nanna warns her that there is 'no luck in refusing a man of the road', but she is ignored.

Pats and Carthalawn certainly make those they curse feel uncomfortable and foolish, but they have no real power and they are jeered at by Thomasheen, Mena and Seán Dóta. As Pats points out, the country is changing and with it the value system the tinkers represent. They are honest and possessed of integrity, but such qualities have no place in the new Ireland Keane describes. Power now rests with the likes of Seán Dóta. The failure of Pats and Carthalawn to affect the outcome of the play reflects the powerlessness of decency, truth, compassion and justice in the world of the text.

Honourable and decent

The various characters in the play are divided in their attitudes towards Pats and Carthalawn. Mena, Thomasheen and Seán Dóta dislike and distrust the travelling men. Thomasheen calls them 'a brace of dirty beggars' and accuses them of 'goin' around criticisin' dacent men an' women'. In reality, Pats and Carthalawn are far more decent and morally upright than those who insult and deride them.

Pats and Carthalawn are on the side of good, which is reflected in the people who side with them in the play. Mike, although he goes along with Thomasheen's plans, is nonetheless delighted when the tinkers curse him in a powerful song, calling him a 'melted amadawn' and wishing that dreadful things may befall him: 'May he screech with awful thirst/May his brains and eyeballs burst.' Mike treats the tinkers with courtesy and generosity throughout the play, which shows that he is a fundamentally decent person, even if he is doing the wrong thing in supporting the match.

Nanna and Liam like and support the pair, and they in turn do all they can to help rescue Sive from her dreadful predicament. They are perceptive enough to see that Liam truly loves Sive while Seán Dóta's interest in her is lustful: ''Tis the flesh of her he do be doting over.' Together with Liam, they devise a plan for the young couple to elope, and Pats delivers Liam's letter containing details of the plan to Nanna, asking her to give it to Sive.

Judges of morality

It is Pats and Carthalawn who have the final say in *Sive*. Their words leave little doubt as to the rights and wrongs of what has happened, and who they hold responsible:

Oh, they murdered lovely Sive,

She would not be a bride,

And they laid her dead, to bury in the clay.

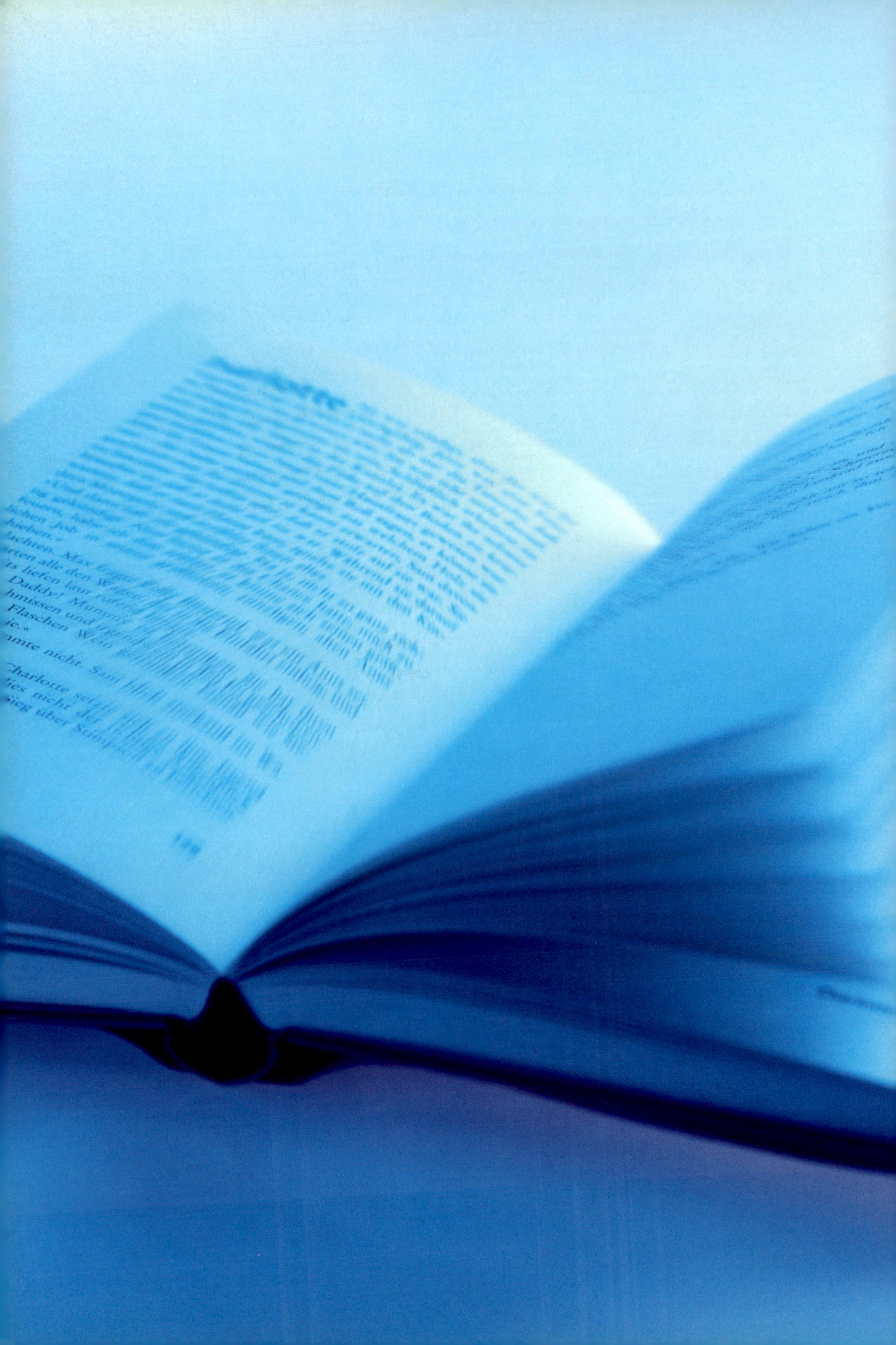

3 The single text

THE SINGLE TEXT

Guide to the Single Text exam section

Paper 2, Ordinary Level: this section is worth **60 marks**

The Single Text is the first section examined in Paper 2. There are a number of different single texts set each year and these are listed on the first page of your exam paper along with the relevant page number.

You are required to study only **one** of these single texts.

Beware: sometimes a book you are studying as part of your Comparative Study will also appear as a Single Text option. It is vitally important to answer the Single Text questions on *Sive* only. If you use your Comparative Study text in the Single Text section, you will not be able to use it in the Comparative Study section.

You are required to know your Single Text in far more detail than you know your Comparative Study texts.

Types of question asked

You will be required to answer **three ten-mark questions** and **one thirty-mark question**. There is no choice in the ten-mark questions; you must answer all of them. There is a choice between three different thirty-mark questions. You need answer only **one** of these.

Ten-mark questions

Character

This is undoubtedly the examiners' favourite type of question. You may be asked to comment on one or more of the main characters and say why they act the way they do in the play.

Relationships

These questions generally focus on the central relationships in the play, all of which are covered in detail in this book.

Plot questions

In these questions you may be asked what happens at a particular point in the text. You must be accurate here. Do not give analysis or personal opinion when answering a question on the plot unless you are asked to do so.

The world of the text/social setting

You may be asked questions about the setting of the play and how the time and place in which they live affects the characters.

Theme or issue

You may be asked to comment on the theme of the text.

An important moment in the text

You may be asked to describe a happy, sad, pleasant, disturbing, violent, frightening, important, amusing, enjoyable or dangerous moment. Remember, when describing this moment, to say **why** it is happy or sad, etc.

The ending

You may be asked to comment on the ending. Was it what you expected? How were things resolved for various characters?

Writer's attitude towards the subject of the play

Be sure you are able to say what this attitude is and how it is conveyed to us by the writing.

Thirty-mark questions

Many of the questions in this section are similar to the ten-mark questions. The principal difference is the length of answer expected. This type of question is effectively a short writing task, similar to the Comprehension Question B answers in Paper 1. You should bear this in mind when planning and writing your answer. The **layout** of the letter or diary entry or whatever you may be asked to do is not as

THE SINGLE TEXT

important as it is in the Comprehension Question B section, but if you are looking for a high grade, you should make an effort to use appropriate language, show an awareness of your audience and generally show an understanding of how such a task should be approached.

As it is a thirty-mark question, you should be aiming to write around six paragraphs, each containing a valid point.

There is an element of personal response here, but be very careful to ensure that your answer is based on the play. There is occasionally some scope for you to use your imagination, but only in the way you express yourself. In other words, if you are asked to pretend you are one of the characters and are writing a diary entry after a significant event, you must be sure to stick to the facts of the event as they are presented in the play. This is a test of your knowledge of the play. Don't be fooled by seemingly vague questions or by the word 'imagine'. The answers must all be based on the Single Text itself and nothing else.

If you are asked for your opinion of the play, try to be positive. You may not like the play but it was chosen as a good example of its genre, and you would be unwise to criticise it.

Character study

This is a very common question, as it is in the ten-mark section. In this question, you may be asked to pretend you are one of the characters in the play, and to write the diary entry he or she might make after a significant event. Or you may be asked whether or not you could live with one of the characters. Another option may be a question requiring you to write a speech defending or prosecuting a certain character. Of course, the question may simply ask you to analyse one of the main characters, but it is more likely to be framed as a short writing task along the lines of those given in Comprehension Question B in Paper 1.

World of the text/setting

You may be asked what differences there are between the world of the text and the world in which you live. Would you like to live in the world of the text? What have you learnt about the world of the text from reading the play? How did the setting/world of the text affect the plot and/or the characters' lives?

Relationships

These questions generally focus on the central relationships in the play.

Review

You may be asked to write an article or a speech in which you give your opinion of the play. In general, you will be asked to present this speech or article to an audience of your peers. In other words, you should be prepared to tell other students what you thought of the play and whether or not you would recommend it to them. Make sure to consider several different aspects of the play when planning your answer. Is the theme one that would appeal to your peers? What about the language? Does the drama move at a fast pace and keep you gripped from start to finish? Are the characters likeable? Could you relate to the issues dealt with in the play? Did you learn anything from the play?

Try to be as positive as you can when answering this question. Refer to the play in every single paragraph.

Report

Here you will have to imagine that you are a reporter, or possibly a police officer, writing a report on an event that has taken place in the play.

Theme or issue

What view of life do you get from the play? Is it uplifting or depressing? Are there life lessons to be learned? What is the author's attitude towards the theme of the play?

THE SINGLE TEXT

An important moment in the text

You may be asked to describe a happy, sad, pleasant, disturbing, violent, frightening, important, amusing, enjoyable or dangerous moment. Remember, when describing this moment, to say **why** it is happy or sad, etc.

Alternative endings

Occasionally, you are asked to imagine how the events in the play might have turned out if characters had made different choices. This is a difficult question to tackle as the temptation to wander far from the text itself can be great. Try to base your answer on the text as far as possible. Try to keep the characters' behaviour in keeping with the way they acted throughout the play.

Important note

The Comparative Study notes in this book are also intended to be used to help Ordinary Level students prepare for the Single Text section of the examination. For example, **themes**, the **world of the text** and **relationships** are also dealt with in the Comparative Study section and all of these are areas which should be covered by anyone studying *Sive* as a Single Text.

Guidelines for answering exam questions

This section is worth **60 marks** and should take you a little less than an hour to complete

When you read the question, underline the key words: **describe, explain, outline,** etc.

Study the question carefully. Try to paraphrase it. What exactly are you being asked? Is the question on plot or character, for example? Is there more than one part to the question? Look for the word 'and'. This can be an indication that there are two parts to the question.

Plan your answer. It is well worth taking the time to do this.

Think in terms of key moments: this will ensure that you refer to the text and will help you to keep the sequence of events in the right order.

Do not, under any circumstances, simply summarise the plot.

Remember that, as a general rule (although you must be guided by the question first and foremost), five marks equals one well-developed point. One well-developed point equals one paragraph. So if a question is worth thirty marks, you should try to make at least six points. You may also wish to include a brief introduction and conclusion.

It cannot be stressed enough that, unless you are specifically asked to do so in a recall question, simply retelling the story will not get you marks. Avoid falling into the trap of simply describing the world of the text without saying what effect it has on the characters' lives.

In order to get high marks, you need to:
- *Answer the question asked (30 per cent).*
- *Make sure every paragraph develops that answer (30 per cent).*
- *Use varied and appropriate language (30 per cent).*
- *Keep an eye on your spelling and grammar (10 per cent).*

Look back over the plan. Does each point you are intending to make answer the question? Is each point backed up by an example from the text? Do the paragraphs flow logically from one to the next?

THE SINGLE TEXT

Past examination questions

Paper 2, Ordinary Level

2010

C. *Sive* – John B. Keane

Answer **all** of the questions.

1. (a) Describe how Mena plans to arrange a match for Sive. (10)

    (b) Do you think that Mike, Mena's husband, is a weak man? Explain your answer. (10)

2. Do you like Sive's grandmother, Nanna Glavin? Explain your answer with reference to the text. (10)

3. Answer **one** of the following: [Each part carries 30 marks]

    (i) Do you agree that Thomasheen Seán Rua is an absolute scoundrel? Support your answer with reference to the play.

    OR

    (ii) Write a piece beginning with one of the following statements:
    - I feel sorry for Sive because …
    - I feel angry with Mena Glavin because …

    OR

    (iii) What arguments would you use to persuade Mena that she should allow Sive to marry Liam Scuab? Support your answer with reference to the text.

Additional sample questions

1. Describe a moment in the play that you found particularly memorable. (10)

2. What is your impression of Seán Dóta? (10)

Sample answers

> 1. (a) Describe how Mena plans to arrange a match for Sive.
>
> 2010 — 10 MARKS

Comment: This question requires you to outline all the steps Mena takes in arranging the match between Sive and Seán Dóta. It is best to approach these steps in chronological order as this will ensure that your answer is well structured.

SAMPLE ANSWER 1

The first step Mena takes is to win Mike over to the idea of a match for Sive. She tells him that they are lucky that anyone wants to marry Sive with 'the slur and the doubt' of her illegitimacy hanging over her. She tries to entice Mike with the promise of a more intimate relationship: 'We will have the house here to ourselves with the oul' woman gone as well.' Finally she mentions the £200 and asks Mike to consider how much easier their lives would be if they had such a sum.

The events are listed in the order in which they took place in the play

That same evening, Seán Dóta and Thomasheen call to the house and Mena sends Sive down to a neighbour's house on an unnecessary errand, accompanied by Seán Dóta. Her true intention is to allow the old man time alone with Sive. However, Sive is repulsed by Seán Dóta and his lecherous ways.

It is essential to quote to support your answer. It is best to weave short, relevant quotes into your sentence rather than reproducing large chunks of the original text

The following week, Mena talks directly to Sive about the match, encouraging her to think of 'the handling of thousands and the fine clothes and the perfumery'. Still Sive resists, so Mena changes tack. Cruelly she tells Sive that she is illegitimate: 'It's time you were told, my girl. You are a bye-child – a common bastard!' She also announces that Sive's schooldays are over and that she cannot share a room with Nanna any longer.

Sive is shattered by all of this, but Mena has one more trick up her sleeve. She knows that Sive loves Liam Scuab and is hoping that they

SIVE 83

THE SINGLE TEXT

Even in a ten-mark question, you should have a clear ending to your answer

may yet be together. Mena forbids Liam from meeting Sive when he calls and she and Mike throw him out of the house. In an act of dreadful cruelty, Mena then tells Sive that Liam called to wish her 'joy and plenty' in her married life and to say that he was 'going away altogether to foreign places'. Sive's spirit is finally broken and she puts up no further resistance to the match. She accepts her lot in passive misery until she is finally driven to such depths of despair that she takes her own life, thus putting an end to Mena's diabolical plotting.

> **10 MARKS — 2010**
>
> 1. (b) Do you think that Mike, Mena's husband, is a weak man? Explain your answer.

Comment: This is a question on character. You should revise the notes on Mike Glavin before attempting to write your own answer.

There is no right or wrong answer to the question. All that matters is that you can make a strong case for your viewpoint, and that you can support each point you make with quotation from or reference to the text.

It is generally easier to go with the most obvious answer. Although two options are given below, there is more evidence to back up the idea that Mike is weak than there is to say that he has much strength of character. Whichever approach you take, be sure not to weaken your argument by pointing out any of Mike's characteristics that contradict the stance you have taken. Mike is not a straightforward character, so when you are planning your answer you will undoubtedly think of points that go against the approach you are taking. Ignore such points.

SAMPLE ANSWER 2 – OPTION 1: MIKE *IS NOT* A WEAK MAN

Opening sentences clearly state the direction of the answer

No, I do not think Mike Glavin is a weak man. He has human failings, certainly, but his actions are understandable in the light of his situation.

Mike is a hardworking man struggling to eke out a living for himself and his family on a poor hill farm. He genuinely wants the best for his niece and has made every effort to comply with his late sister's wishes that he raise Sive like a father and see that she is well educated. I believe this shows strength and determination on Mike's part, particularly when his wife is set against Sive and resents what she sees as the preferential treatment the girl receives.

Personal response: 'I' is required when answering a question that asks your opinion

While Mike knows that the match between Sive and Seán Dóta is a bad idea, he is so concerned about her relationship with Liam that he is eager to see her married off safely, and therefore agrees to the match, albeit reluctantly. He fears that Liam will take advantage of Sive and leave her a single parent like her own mother. He does not believe that Sive's father, Liam's cousin, ever intended to marry Sive's mother. It is understandable that Mike should be wary of Liam and concerned lest his relationship with Sive ends in shame and sadness. Mike tells Nanna that if Sive marries Seán Dóta, she will still be 'only a girl and lucky, not a woman who will have been thinking of men'.

I believe that Mike is in an impossible position in his household. If he agrees to the match, he upsets his mother and his niece. If he opposes it, he upsets his wife. In the end, Mike sides with Mena. As he explains to Nanna: 'A man's wife will always be his wife, let them both be what they will.' It is not weakness that makes Mike go along with Mena's plan, but rather loyalty to her and a determination to keep Sive from ending up like her mother. I do not agree with Mike's choices, but I think he shows strength, possibly misguided, in his determination to see the match through to the end.

SAMPLE ANSWER 3 – OPTION 2: MIKE *IS* A WEAK MAN

Yes, I believe Mike Glavin is a weak man who is partly responsible for driving his niece, Sive, to her death.

Revise the section on Mike's character and look for key, descriptive words to support your viewpoint

When Mike first hears of the proposed match, he is outraged, saying that he could never allow such a thing and that it would be 'like tossing the white flower of the canavaun on to the manure heap'. However, he soon caves in to the relentless pressure from Mena and

THE SINGLE TEXT

This point shows that you have analysed the events of the play and reached your own conclusions

Thomasheen and allows himself to be swayed by the thought of the £200: 'The money is a great temptation.'

Even though he knows in his heart that the match is wrong and he is fully aware that Sive is miserable, Mike does nothing to stop it. He comes across as an ineffectual man who is easily browbeaten by his aggressive and determined wife.

Mike's insistence on clinging to the idea that Liam is unreliable and unsuitable for Sive is, I believe, another example of his weakness. Just because Liam's cousin got Sive's mother pregnant out of wedlock does not mean that Liam will do the same to Sive. Mike's refusal to believe that Liam is honourable says more about him than it does about Liam.

If Mike genuinely wants to protect Sive from lecherous men, he should certainly not allow Seán Dóta near her. He does, however, and consents to the pair going down the road together in the dark, even though Seán Dóta is clearly only interested in Sive's youthful beauty. Even when Liam tells Mike that he has heard Seán Dóta talking about the things he will do to Sive 'before she is much older', Mike does nothing.

A strong ending is appropriate when you are making your case

I cannot respect Mike Glavin. He does not have sufficient courage to stand up for what he knows to be right and he permits his niece to be sold to an old man, although he knows that she and Liam Scuab love one another dearly and want to be married. I do not believe that Mike has a single redeeming feature: he is simply a weak man ruled by greed and cowardice.

10 MARKS · 2010

2. Do you like Sive's grandmother, Nanna Glavin?
   Explain your answer with reference to the text.

Comment: As with 1(b) above, this is a question about character. Again, there is no right or wrong answer. The examiner does not need to agree with your opinion in order to give you a high grade. You simply have to make a good case.

86 NIFTY NOTES

SAMPLE ANSWER 4 – OPTION 1: YES, I LIKE NANNA GLAVIN

Yes, I like Nanna Glavin. She is a feisty, tough old lady who loyally stands by her beloved granddaughter and does everything in her power to prevent the match between Sive and Seán Dota going ahead. Nanna's life is not an easy one. She is constantly bullied and insulted by Mena. Still, Nanna does not take the insults lying down. When Mena taunts her, saying that her hidden pipe will some day cause her to 'go off in a big black ball of smoke and ashes', Nanna's spirited and amusing response, 'If I do, 'tis my prayer the wind will blow me in your direction and I'll have the satisfaction of taking you with me', endears her to me.

Strong, decisive opening which shows the points that will be explored in this answer

Her love for Sive is Nanna's most admirable quality. She, alone in the family, wants what is best for Sive, and supports the girl in her relationship with Liam Scuab.

Remember to link all points back to the question. If you say something about Nanna, you must then explain why this makes you like her

When she hears of the proposed match, Nanna is appalled. Bravely, she stands up to Mena and Thomasheen, telling them that the match is 'the devil's work' and that there has been 'a hatchery of sin' in the house since they began plotting. She is bullied and threatened for her trouble, but still sticks to her assertion.

This shows good knowledge of the text and a level of analysis

Nanna continues to fight for Sive and Liam, begging Mike to reconsider the match and telling him that Liam Scuab would make a good husband for Sive: 'There is a sweet thing in their love.' I respect Nanna's strength of character and her unswerving loyalty to the young couple.

It would be easy to criticise Nanna for handing Liam's letter to Mike, but in her defence she does not believe she can give it to Sive herself: 'They will be watching for me to leave my room and they would see me giving it to her.' Her plan has merit; Mike does indeed intend to give the letter to Sive but it is intercepted and destroyed by Thomasheen.

Nanna may have failed in her bid to save Sive, but she did her best right up to the end. Her heartbreak at the end of the play when she weeps over Sive's body reinforces my belief that Nanna is a deeply loyal, loving woman who deserves our admiration and respect.

Clear ending

THE SINGLE TEXT

SAMPLE ANSWER 5 – OPTION 2: NO, I DO NOT LIKE NANNA GLAVIN

No, I do not like Nanna Glavin. While she has some admirable qualities, such as her love for Sive, I think Nanna's hatred for Mena creates an acrimonious atmosphere in the house and is partly responsible for Mena's dislike of Sive and her eagerness to be rid of both her and Nanna.

Mena may be unpleasant to Nanna, but the old woman is exceptionally hurtful to Mena in return. She frequently taunts her with her childlessness, saying that she is 'as dry as the hobs of hell' and pointing out that all the local women of Mena's age have children by now. This is not only cruel, but also foolish and selfish behaviour. Nanna provokes Mena constantly, and thus is in no position to plead Sive's case with her when the issue of the match arises.

Nanna refuses to accept Mena's role as female head of the household and does her best to come between Mena and Mike, although she denies it. It is hypocritical of Nanna to tell Mike that she does not want 'to spoil your home and put ye fighting', while at the same time calling Mena a 'greasy bitch', a 'pauperised wretch' and a 'hungry sow' who has brought 'a curse of evil' on the house. I don't think that this is a fair way to talk to her son about his wife, nor do I think that it makes Mike more likely to listen to Nanna when she asks him to reconsider the match.

There is one final reason I do not like Nanna, and that is her foolishness in giving Liam's letter to Mike. She claims she does this because she has no opportunity to deliver it to Sive, but I find this hard to believe. Indeed, she does not even try to do so, but hands it over to Mike almost as soon as she gets it. Sive never receives the letter and, in misery and despair, takes her own life.

Although I feel sorry for Nanna when she weeps over Sive's body at the end of the play, I hold her partly responsible for the tragedy and therefore cannot like her.

3. **(i) Do you agree that Thomasheen Seán Rua is an absolute scoundrel? Support your answer with reference to the play.**

2010 — 30 MARKS

Q. *What sort of task is this?*

A. This is a persuasive piece. You are making your case for liking or disliking Thomasheen.

Q. *What should the content be?*

A. This is an analysis of Thomasheen's character. The word 'absolute' before scoundrel gives you the opportunity to say that you do not think he is completely bad, if you wish. While there are no right and wrong answers when you are asked for your opinion, it would be next to impossible to argue convincingly that Thomasheen is anything but a scoundrel. To do so would be to show a poor understanding of the text and the playwright's intentions in creating such a character.

Q. *Who is my audience?*

A. There is no audience specified in this question. When this is the case, try to imagine that you are writing for your own teacher, and err on the side of caution. You will not be penalised for being too formal in your writing, but you may be penalised for using a chatty tone when it is inappropriate to do so. Think of the approach you use for your Comprehension Question B answers in Paper 1 when planning your response to the thirty-mark question in Paper 2.

Q. *What register should I use?*

A. See above.

SAMPLE ANSWER 6 – OPTION 1:
THOMASEEN *IS* AN ABSOLUTE SCOUNDREL

Yes, I believe Thomasheen Seán Rua is an absolute scoundrel. He is an amoral, greedy, unscrupulous, cowardly, misogynistic man who is a destructive force from the moment he appears in the play. Even the stage directions predispose us to dislike the man. He is described as a

You should outline your reasons for disliking Thomasheen in the opening paragraph

THE SINGLE TEXT

shabby, unshaven man who is 'shifty-looking, ever on his guard'.

The first and most obvious reason for despising Thomasheen is the fact that he is prepared to sell Sive to a lecherous old farmer. He knows quite well that Seán Dóta has no love for Sive and merely lusts after her. He tells Mena that Seán Dóta has seen Sive cycling to the convent each day and that when he speaks of her 'he have the mouth half-open'. He goes on to say that Seán Dóta has 'the mad mind for women breaking out through him like the tetter with no cure for it'. I find it amoral and disgusting that Thomasheen should be prepared to force Sive into marriage with such a man.

Personal response is required in an answer which asks for your opinion

Thomasheen has no interest in anyone's happiness but his own. He uses every means at his disposal to bring about the match. He never asks Sive how she feels about it, but approaches Mena and persuades her to get Sive to agree to the marriage. He advises Mena to be cruel to Sive, telling her to use Sive's illegitimacy as a weapon and to threaten to 'bell-rag her through the parish if she goes against you'.

Each paragraph should answer the question asked

Thomasheen's willingness to destroy people's relationships and lives if it will serve his purposes is proof of what an absolute scoundrel he is. From the moment he enters the Glavin house he is a destructive force. He uses the existing tensions between the family members to his advantage, pretending to sympathise with Mena when she expresses her dislike of Sive and Nanna, and advising her to get rid of the pair of them by making Nanna part of the match. He knows Mike is against the marriage, but he doesn't care. He tells Mena that she should use her sexual wiles to manipulate her husband into agreeing to the marriage: 'Aren't ye in the one bed sleeping? Ye will have yeer own talk.' He realises Liam Scuab is a threat, so he plays on Mike's fear of Sive ending up like her mother by warning him that the young people are meeting secretly. He knows that this will spur Mike on to marrying Sive off quickly before she can get into any trouble.

Links between paragraphs help your answer to flow well. Phrases like 'yet another' show the examiner that your answer is well planned. A similar effect can be achieved by beginning paragraphs with phrases such as 'The first reason …', 'Finally …', etc

Yet another reason to dislike Thomasheen is his cowardly nature. He bullies Nanna horribly, but never in front of Mike. He threatens the vulnerable old woman with the county home and tells her a horrific story of a woman just like her who died in torment and madness because she was not allowed to smoke her pipe in the home. Thomasheen is delighted to see that 'the old woman is tiring' after all the abuse and insults he and Mena hurl at her.

Thomasheen has no understanding of love, decency or goodness. He seems to dislike women and compares them to animals that need to be whipped and harnessed until they submit. Anyone who sees life and love differently is scorned by this dreadful man. He mocks Liam's beautiful sentiments in the letter he writes to Sive, and scorns Pats and Carthalawn because they 'have no liking' for the matchmaker and his manipulative, greedy ways.

There is no doubt that Thomasheen is responsible for Sive's death. His diabolical scheming and utterly unscrupulous behaviour in forcing her to accept a match with a man she loathes drive the innocent girl to despair and suicide. Yet even when he sees her body carried into the house, Thomasheen acts in a contemptible manner. He sidles quickly out of the door, leaving the Glavins' house in the same furtive, underhand way he entered it, and leaving death and heartbreak in his wake.

By the end of your answer you should have given evidence to support all the points you raised in your introductory paragraph

SAMPLE ANSWER 7 – OPTION 2:
THOMASHEEN *IS NOT* AN ABSOLUTE SCOUNDREL

Comment: As was stated in the introduction to the previous sample answer to this question, it is difficult to argue that Thomasheen is anything but a scoundrel. However, if you focus on the word 'absolute' in the question, you could argue that there are, perhaps, excuses for Thomasheen's behaviour and some hints that he is not bad through and through. Still, this is a difficult approach to take and you would need to have a thorough knowledge of the details of the play and the characters, as well as an ability to argue convincingly even when you don't have a good case. There are advantages to attempting a tricky option like this, if you feel you can handle it, not least because the majority of students will have taken the easier option so your answer will stand out and may catch the examiner's attention.

THE SINGLE TEXT

The introduction outlines the approach the answer is going to take by focusing on the word 'absolute'

While there is no doubt that Thomasheen is a scoundrel, I do not believe he is an absolute scoundrel. His behaviour may seem despicable and inexcusable, and much of it is, but I feel that he is also a victim of the time he lives in and of the poverty and misery of his upbringing.

There is no point in defending all of Thomasheen's behaviour, but you can try to make the reader see things from his point of view whenever possible, and perhaps sympathise with his situation

Thomasheen is 'fortyish', and has been a matchmaker for many years. When he was a young man, matchmaking was quite common in rural Ireland and was seen as a sensible and practical way of bringing people together. However, by the 1950s it had all but died out and the younger generation in the play view it with distaste and bewilderment. Sive and Liam agree that it is 'horrible', but even then, Liam acknowledges that some people say 'it is necessary in country places'. It is easy for modern readers to scorn Thomasheen for trying to arrange marriages, but I feel a certain sympathy for him in that his job, which was once quite respected, is now regarded with derision. When Pats Bocock and Carthalawn first visit the Glavin house, Thomasheen tells Nanna and Mena that they dislike him because he has 'great call at the matchmaking'. If matchmaking dies out completely, as seems inevitable, Thomasheen will be completely destitute. This may go some way towards explaining his desperation to earn enough of a lump sum to enable him to have a secure future.

If we accept that Thomasheen's way of earning a living is not something for which he should automatically be censured, we must look closely at the match he intends to make between Sive and Seán Dóta. Our first reaction, like that of Mena and Mike, is incredulity. It seems dreadful to expect a young girl to marry such an old man, and we may be inclined to look down on Thomasheen for suggesting it. However, he does appear to believe that once Sive is reconciled to the match, she will probably be happy. He tells Mena that Seán Dóta 'would spoil her, I tell you. There is good reward for all concerned in it.'

Thomasheen's view of marriage may seem mercenary and unromantic, but we learn that he has been hardened and embittered by his own experiences in this area. He confides in Mena and Mike that he did once love a girl, but that he couldn't marry her as his father committed suicide and the young Thomasheen had to spend the money he had saved for the marriage on the funeral. Now he is single and lonely. It is hard not to feel sorry for him when he tells Mena: 'I know what it is to be alone in a house when the only word you will hear is a sigh, the sigh of the fire in the hearth dying, with no human words to warm you.' If he can bring about this match, Thomasheen will finally have enough money to enable him to marry a local widow woman. While this does not excuse his trying to force Sive into marriage with Seán Dóta, it does explain it somewhat, and shows us a more vulnerable and pathetic side to a man we may otherwise regard as an out-and-out rogue.

You should refer back to the question regularly in your answer, to ensure that you stay on track. You do not need to use the exact wording of the question: here 'out-and-out rogue' replaces 'absolute scoundrel'

It is not only when he is admitting his loneliness or lost opportunities for love that we see there is more to Thomasheen than his unpleasant manner and unscrupulous actions may suggest. When he mocks Mike for claiming that Sive is too romantic to marry for money, Thomasheen reveals an understanding of the very romance he derides, asking Mena if Mike ever runs to her when he comes home to give her 'a big smohawnach of a kiss and tell you that the length of the day was like the length of a million years while he was separated from you'. This, and the other examples of romantic behaviour he lists to Mena and Mike, show us that Thomasheen does, or did once, understand true love on some level. However, he has been so badly scarred by his own thwarted effort to marry for love that he now refuses to think this way and instead jeers and mocks those who do.

I think that, rather than being a complete scoundrel, Thomasheen is a damaged, sad man who has lost all hope of true love in his own life, and thus has a cynical and mercenary view of the world. Certainly, his behaviour is reprehensible by and large, and he is undoubtedly a scoundrel, but not an absolute one. Anyone who cannot see the misery Thomasheen has endured and cannot feel some sympathy for him in his impoverished, lonely life is just as callous and unfeeling as they accuse him of being.

As this is a difficult viewpoint to defend, you will have to use reasonably forceful language to make your case, particularly in the conclusion. In this instance, power of persuasion needs to triumph over the truth

THE SINGLE TEXT

30 MARKS | 2010

3. (ii) Write a piece beginning with one of the following statements:
 – I feel sorry for Sive because …
 – I feel angry with Mena Glavin because …

Q. What sort of task is this?
A. This is a persuasive piece in which you make a case.

Q. What should the content be?
A. You should write five or six reasons for feeling angry with Mena or sorry for Sive.

Q. Who is my audience?
A. There is no audience specified in this question. When this is the case, try to imagine that you are writing for your own teacher, and err on the side of caution. You will not be penalised for being too formal in your writing, but you may be penalised for using a chatty tone when it is inappropriate to do so.

Q. What register should I use?
A. See above.

SAMPLE ANSWER 8 – OPTION 1: I FEEL SORRY FOR SIVE …

The opening paragraph states the reasons for feeling sorry for Sive. These will be developed throughout the answer

I feel sorry for Sive because she is an innocent victim of unscrupulous, greedy, amoral people. She has, as Liam says, 'a 'pure spirit' but she is no match for the forces of evil that surround her. My heart goes out to this poor orphaned child who is betrayed by the people who should care for her.

Personal response: 'I' is required throughout when answering a question that asks for your opinion

Sive is an attractive character, and I empathised with her from the beginning of the play. She is gentle and refined, never rising to her aunt's jibes about her education or the secrecy surrounding her parentage.

I think it must be very difficult for Sive, growing up without a mother or a father and being raised by an aunt who hates and resents her. Mena does not have a good word to say to Sive, and addresses her harshly except when she is trying to win the girl around to the idea of the match. That Sive is used to being insulted and abused by Mena is clear from her bewilderment when Mena, in an effort to soften Sive up prior to introducing the conversation about Seán Dóta, offers her a cup of tea and a slice of cake on her return home from school. Sive's astonishment at being treated nicely is pitiful.

Even though she is around eighteen years of age, Sive has little control of her own destiny. She loves Liam Scuab, and he her, but she is forbidden from seeing him because her uncle disapproves of the young man. It would be hard not to feel great sympathy for Sive when it is revealed that she has to sneak out to the bog at night if she wants to meet the man she loves.

> *It is a good idea to write your points in chronological order, whenever possible. This ensures that your answer has a clear beginning, middle and end*

Poor Sive has no hope from the moment Mena decides to sell her to Seán Dóta. What happens to Sive from then on is heartbreaking. She is isolated from the people who love and care for her and she is mercilessly hounded until her spirit is broken and she agrees to the match.

Sive is loved by three people: Liam, Nanna and Mike. It is this love and support that Mena and Thomasheen are determined to remove so that Sive will be completely at their mercy. I can only imagine how Sive must feel when she realises that her uncle Mike, who has been, in Nanna's words, 'better than a father to her' is going to stand by and allow her to be sold to a man she despises. Her isolation and misery is increased when she is separated from Nanna and told that she must now sleep in the room beside Mena and Mike, so that she has no chance to be alone with her beloved grandmother.

Everything that is good in Sive's life is gradually taken away from her. Although I may complain about school from time to time, I felt dreadfully sorry for Sive when Mena announces that she is finished with education and cannot go to the convent any more.

Mena's cruelty seems to know no bounds. My heart went out to Sive when I read the scene in which Mena tells Sive the lie that Liam accepts the idea of her marrying Seán Dóta, wishes her well and is leaving the area for good. Sive's cry of despair, 'Oh! Liam could never do a thing like that', is dreadfully sad.

    The worst betrayal of all, and the part of the play that never fails to affect me, is Mike allowing Liam's letter to Sive to be read and destroyed. He never tells her its contents, and so Sive never learns that Liam loves her still and that there is hope of an escape. That Sive should take her own life in the belief that she has been abandoned by everyone, but particularly Liam, is truly heartbreaking.

    It is impossible not to be deeply moved by the final image in the play, that of Nanna weeping over the body of her dead granddaughter. I shared her sorrow for the tragic girl who was 'hunted to her grave' by evil people.

SAMPLE ANSWER 9 – OPTION 2: I FEEL ANGRY WITH MENA …

> *The most obvious thing to focus on in this answer is the part Mena plays in Sive's death, but if you only talk about that, you will soon run out of things to say. Try to think of all the aspects of Mena's behaviour that you dislike*

I feel angry with Mena Glavin because she is the person who is ultimately responsible for destroying Sive's life and, with it, the happiness of those around her. The thing about Mena's behaviour that disgusts me most is that she has several opportunities to make her family happy, but never takes those chances, instead seizing on the options that bring nothing but misery and heartbreak.

    Certainly, Mena has never had it easy. She came from a poor family, and had to struggle to make enough money to enable her to marry Mike. Then she had to cope with infertility, an illegitimate niece and a resentful mother-in-law. However, Mena does nothing to make

> *A personal response is required in an answer of this kind. Be sure to use the word 'I' regularly, and refer back to the question as often as you can. Try to vary your vocabulary so you are not saying 'I am angry' the whole time. If you use words and phrases like 'despicable', 'monstrously selfish' and 'utterly contemptible', this will show your opinion of Mena quite clearly*

life happier for herself, Mike, Nanna or Sive, and I find her behaviour despicable. Instead of showing some sympathy for the motherless baby in her new home, she says she had to contend with 'a dirty brat of an orphan bawling in the corner'. She fights viciously and hatefully with Nanna, and treats her husband with scorn, calling him 'a poor amadawn'. Nanna does not help the situation, and fights Mena quite openly, but that is no excuse for Mena's treatment of the older woman. When Nanna calls the match 'the devil's work', Mena is so incensed that she threatens the old woman with destitution and even physical violence.

Nanna does provoke Mena several times in the play, but Sive is nothing but polite and respectful to her aunt. Still, Mena persists in belittling her, mocking her for her 'high notions' and resenting everything Sive has, from her educational opportunities to the simplest things such as a cup of creamy milk: 'The top of the tank for her ladyship!' If Mena were to treat those around her more kindly, I think the atmosphere in the Glavin house would be greatly improved.

While it could be argued that Mena had little choice when it came to sharing the house with Nanna and Sive, she married Mike of her own free will, and I think her treatment of him is appalling. She jeers at him, calling him a 'man of straw' when he objects to the match between Sive and Seán Dóta, and she connives with Thomasheen behind his back. Mike works hard to support his family, yet Mena seems to have little or no respect for him.

Don't forget to quote to support the points you are making. It can be easy to overlook this when you are caught up in arguing your case, but quotes are essential

The only time Mena is kind to anyone seems to be when she wants something from them. Once she has decided to marry Sive to Seán Dóta, she does her best to win the girl around to the match, trying to persuade her that it will be worth it when she is rich and comfortable. When this fails, she reverts back to her usual, cruel self, telling Sive that she is nothing but 'a bye-child' and that her father never loved her mother. This makes me very angry indeed, as the cruel lie hurts Sive deeply. However, it is Mena's lie about Liam that I think is the most terrible aspect of her plan to arrange the match. Sive and Liam are deeply in love, but this means nothing to Mena. She is determined to break Sive's spirit, and does so in a truly dreadful way. She tells Sive that Liam called to wish her well in her married life, and to say that he was leaving the area for good. Sive's heart is broken by this, and she runs to her room, crying. Far from feeling any regret, Mena is grimly satisfied: 'There 'tis all now settled and no more to it.'

I find Mena's selling of her niece to a lecherous old man utterly contemptible. She knows quite well that the girl is miserable but she doesn't care. She is an intelligent woman and she is well aware that she is ruining Sive's life, as well as causing great pain to Liam, Mike and Nanna. This monstrously selfish behaviour makes me despise Mena.

THE SINGLE TEXT

Sive loses all her vitality as the play progresses, but Mena thrives on the thought of the match, and even steals some of the money intended for Sive's wedding clothes. There seem to be no depths she will not plumb.

The conclusion should refer back to the opening paragraph

There is no redemption for Mena, in my eyes. She may be shocked and horrified by Sive's death, but she does not appear grief-stricken. Liam's violent anger as he condemns Mena accurately reflects my feelings as I watched the events unfold. When the normally controlled Liam calls Mena a 'horrible, filthy bitch' who 'hunted the poor little girl to her grave', I echo his sentiments. Even when he raises his hand to strike Mena, I cannot blame him in the slightest. Mena Glavin's role in the death of an innocent girl, and her blighting of the happiness of everyone around her, fills me with nothing but anger and disgust.

---

30 MARKS | 2010

3. (iii) What arguments would you use to persuade Mena that she should allow Sive to marry Liam Scuab? Support your answer with reference to the text.

Q. *What sort of task is this?*
A. This is a persuasive piece.

Q. *What should the content be?*
A. You should try to think of five or six reasons why Mena should allow Sive to marry Liam. Your answer should be based on a knowledge of Mena's character and what motivates her.

Q. *Who is my audience?*
A. There is no audience specified in this question. When this is the case, try to imagine that you are writing for your own teacher, and err on the side of caution. You will not be penalised for being too formal in your writing, but you may be penalised for using a chatty tone when it is inappropriate to do so.

Q. *What register should I use?*
A. See above.

SAMPLE ANSWER 10

I think that persuading Mena to agree to Sive marrying Liam Scuab would be a difficult task, but I would do my best to use my knowledge of her character and what motivates her when pleading my case.

Reasons for each argument are based on knowledge of the text and of Mena's character

Mena is a selfish character who shows little interest in the feelings of others, but I would make at least one attempt to appeal to her better nature, even though I would not be very optimistic about my chances of success. I would point out to Mena that although she has no great love or romance in her life, she should give Sive the chance to have a better, happier marriage. I would sympathise with Mena's position when she married Mike in order to escape her desperately poor family, but I would tell her that Sive is in a very different position and that she has found someone who both loves her and is able to provide for her since he is working as a carpenter.

Next, I would remind Mena that Sive does not have the same desire for wealth and security that she does. Mena may think that any girl would want a man, however unappealing, who had 'twenty cows, a farm free of debt' and plenty of money, but Sive is not interested in any of that. It is wrong, I would say, to expect others to see things our way and to force them to do things they do not want.

Even in an answer like this, you should quote whenever possible

If these arguments failed, and I think they may well do so, considering how hard and unromantic Mena is, I would appeal directly to Mena's self-interest. I would point out pragmatically that whether Sive marries Liam or Seán Dóta, she will be out of the house and out of Mena's way. Liam is a good and kind man who would probably be happy to take Nanna with him, I would argue, so Mena would get her wish to be 'clear and clane of the pair of 'em'. In fact, she would probably be rid of them sooner and would be sure they would never return, whereas if Sive is forced into a match with Seán Dóta, there is no guarantee that she will go through with it or that she will stay with him for ever.

This shows a level of analysis of the text and an ability to extract knowledge and apply it to hypothetical situations

I would also remind Mena that Mike is against the match and that if Sive is forced to marry against her will and is deeply unhappy, Mike

THE SINGLE TEXT

will probably resent Mena and there will be great tension in the house. This unpleasant atmosphere will be exacerbated by the fact that there will only be the two of them in the house when Sive and Nanna leave, so they will have nobody to talk to but one another.

Finally, and if all else failed, I would ask Mena if she really wants Sive living the high life just down the hill from her old home? Mena may make £200 from the match, but that will be nothing compared to the money Sive will have if she marries Seán Dóta. He has already hinted that he will buy her a motor car. Mena may have urged Sive to picture herself driving to church every week with her 'head in the air', looking pityingly at the poorer women of the locality, but has Mena considered that she may be one of the 'poor oinsheachs' Sive looks down on? Could Mena really bear to see the niece she dislikes so much getting even higher notions than she has already? Mena herself has told Sive that if she marries the old man she will have 'the handling of thousands and the fine clothes and the perfumery'. I would say that if Sive marries Liam, a young carpenter, she will be provided for but will not be in a position to lord it over Mena.

The conclusion reflects the opening and does not introduce any new points

While it would not be an easy task to win Mena around to the idea of abandoning the match between Sive and Seán Dóta, I think that the combination of all of these arguments might just do the trick.

> **10 MARKS** — **SAMPLE QUESTION**: Describe a moment in the play that you found particularly memorable.

Comment: The obvious moment here is the final one in which Liam appears, carrying Sive's body into the house. Remember to read the question carefully. You were asked why you found the scene memorable, so be sure that you refer to that point regularly.

SAMPLE ANSWER 11

The introduction states clearly why the moment is memorable

The moment in the play I found most memorable takes place shortly after Mena discovers that Sive is missing from her room. Events unfold with

100 NIFTY NOTES

alarming swiftness from this point on, and I found myself on the edge of my seat, filled with a mixture of dread that the despairing Sive may have done something drastic, and hope that perhaps she had somehow managed to elope with Liam after all.

Any hopes are dashed, however, when Pats Bocock mentions that he saw a girl running 'across the bog near the end of the cutaway where the deep holes do be'. His words, and Mena's terrified reaction to them, lead us to fear the worst. I found Mena's hysteria particularly striking, as until this point in the play she has never seemed to be afraid of anything or anyone. Her terror is infectious and her uncharacteristic behaviour makes this scene gripping.

Words and phrases like 'striking', 'her terror is infectious', and 'gripping' show that this moment is one which has a great effect on the audience and is therefore unforgettable

Liam's entrance, carrying Sive's dead body, is utterly compelling. The stage directions here add to the effect and ensure that it is a moment in the play I will never forget. Dramatically, he carries Sive's dripping body over to the table, which is centre stage. There is silence, and then Pats sweeps the ware onto the floor where it smashes. I jumped when this happened on stage and my heart raced. When Liam called for a cloth to dry Sive's hair and began to tell the story of chasing her in vain as she ran across the bog in despair, I was transfixed. His grief, and his fury at Mena held me spellbound. Like Mena's earlier hysteria, it is Liam's uncharacteristic behaviour that is so striking. His normal control is gone, and his anger and even his threat to strike Mena make this moment unforgettable. For him to behave this way shows just how strongly he feels and makes this moment one that comes to mind whenever I think of the play. The sadness and grief that follows simply consolidates the tragedy of this poignant and affecting scene.

Reference to staging is a good idea when answering a question of this sort

Personal response, showing the effect the moment had on you, is appropriate

---

SAMPLE QUESTION — 10 MARKS

What is your impression of Seán Dóta?

Comment: You should refer to the character sketch on Seán Dóta in this book when planning your answer. As it is a ten-mark question, two or three aspects of his personality should be plenty.

THE SINGLE TEXT

SAMPLE ANSWER 12

Introduction briefly outlines the points that will be developed as the answer progresses

The impression I get of Seán Dóta is an overwhelmingly negative one. He is a lecherous, mean-spirited old man who is totally unsuitable as a match for a young girl like Sive.

Before we ever meet the elderly farmer, we are predisposed to dislike him. Thomasheen describes how he has seen Sive cycling to school each day and has become 'greatly taken by her'. Clearly, it is only her youth and beauty that have attracted him as there is no mention of his ever having spoken to her. Even Mena is shocked when she hears who the suitor is, and Mike is appalled, describing him as 'a worn, exhausted little lurgadawn of a man'.

Short quotes woven into the sentence help to support your point

When Seán Dóta visits the Glavins for the first time in the play, our unfavourable impressions are reinforced. His irritating false modesty and little half-laugh when he speaks soon grate on the nerves. It is clear that he has nothing in common with Sive, calling poets 'thieves' who are 'filled with roguery' and attempting to impress her with a nonsensical, rather horrifying children's rhyme about a young boy who is hanged for stealing from his mother and is then buried in dung. Sive is repulsed by him, and resists the suggestion that he walk down the road with her to a neighbour's house. He accompanies her nonetheless and makes a violent pass at her, much to her distress. This confirms the impression that he is a lustful old man who is only interested in Sive for one thing.

If you discuss a moment in the play, be sure to link it back to the question. The final sentence of this paragraph does that

Even though Seán Dóta pays handsomely for Sive, he is a mean-spirited man who begrudges the tinkers any charity: 'How soft you have it! Money for nothing, how are you?' He sees Sive as a commodity, and when his investment comes to nothing at the end of the play, he shows no grief for the death of the girl he was to marry, but sneaks furtively out of the house, proving that he had no affection for Sive at all. There is nothing attractive about Seán Dóta from start to finish of this play.

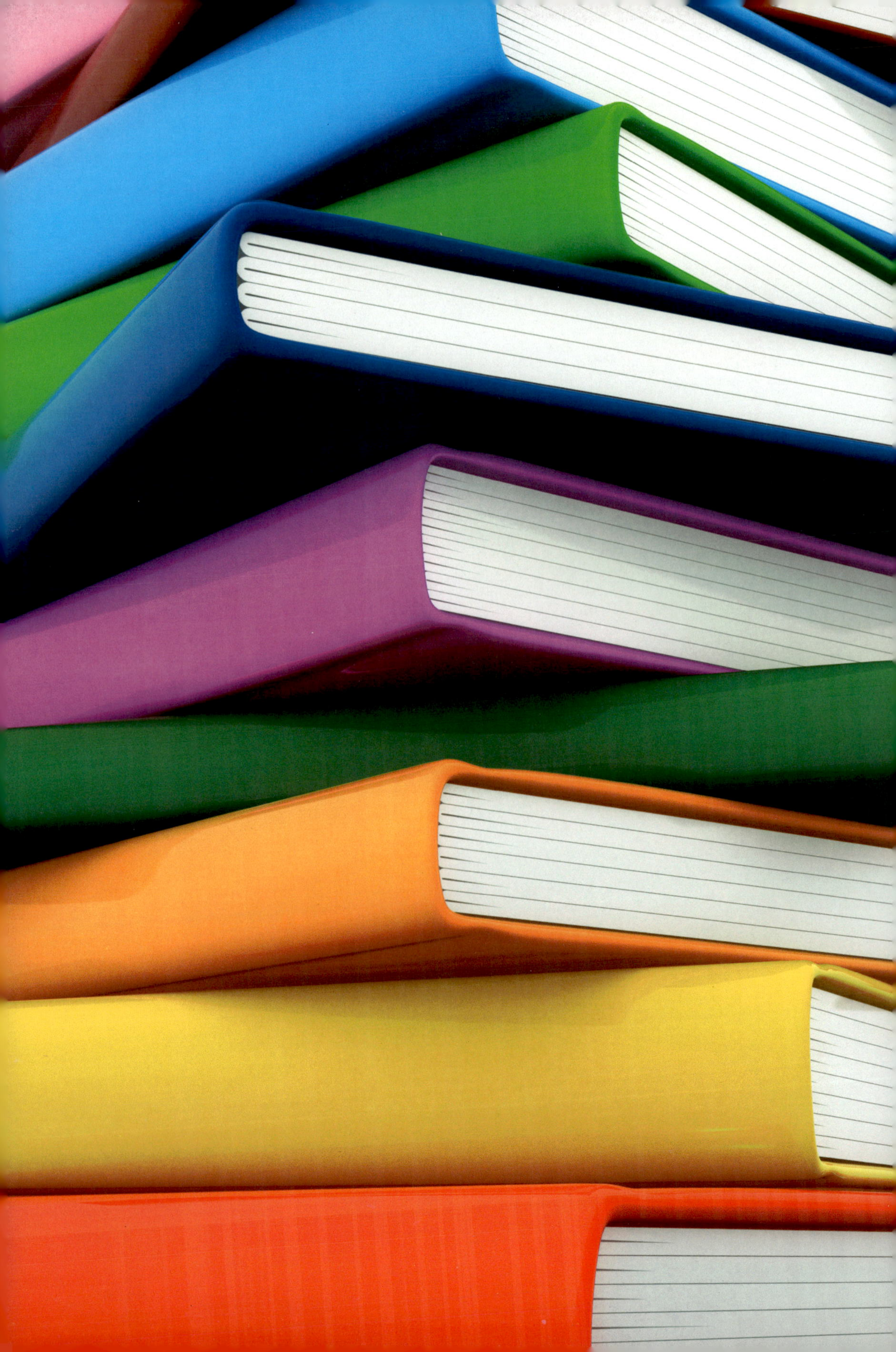

The comparative study

4

THE COMPARATIVE STUDY

Sive

In this chapter you will find comprehensive notes on using *Sive* as a text for your Comparative Study. Each of the comparative modes for Higher Level and Ordinary Level is covered. As the modes change each year, it is important to check which modes apply to the year you will be sitting your Leaving Certificate.

Some of the modes for Higher and Ordinary Level overlap. Where this is the case, one set of notes is given for the two modes.

It is very important to be able to compare the texts you are studying, but you should also bear in mind that at both Higher and Ordinary Level you will usually have the option of answering a thirty-mark question on **one** of the texts.

These notes are designed as a reference guide to help students to put together their own Comparative Study essays. In some cases, headings and bullet points are used for clarity and to make revision easier, but students should not use either in their answers.

There is a certain amount of overlap between the comparative modes, particularly in relation to key moments, but this is inevitable. A key moment can show aspects of the central relationship, the literary genre and the cultural context, for example. As you will only be answering on one mode in the examination, this overlap is not a problem.

In this book, key moments are woven into the Comparative Study notes. As a key moment is described, its relevance to the mode is discussed and explored in detail. Remember, you should never discuss an event in your chosen text without linking it to the point you are making.

Important note

The Comparative Study notes in this book are also intended to be used to help Ordinary Level students prepare for the Single Text section of the examination. For example, **themes**, **the world of the text** (cultural context/social setting) and **relationships** are dealt with in the Comparative Study section, and all of these are areas that should be covered by anyone studying *Sive* as a Single Text.

THE COMPARATIVE STUDY

Literary Genre

Higher Level

Past questions on this mode of comparison have tended to focus on the following:

- *How memorable characters are created in the text*
- *How emotional power is created in the text*
- *The use of setting as an important feature of storytelling*
- *Aspects of narrative and how they contribute to your response to the text*
- *How powerful moments add to the story in the text*
- *How the unexpected contributes to the story*
- *The different ways in which the story is told in the texts you have chosen.*

Point of view

There is no one point of view presented in *Sive*. We are not told what emotions to have, but are instead allowed to form our own opinions on the characters and their actions. Such an objective method of telling the story may seem a little impersonal, but in fact the opposite is true. We are drawn into the world of the text and we must use our own judgement rather than passively accepting the judgement of the author. We may even change our mind about the characters a number of times as the play progresses. Thomasheen Seán Rua, for example, appears to be wholly without feeling when we meet him first, but when we hear his story of lost love we are perhaps more inclined to view him sympathetically, even if only for a short time.

Social realism

Sive is a realistic play that presents an accurate picture of life in rural

Ireland in the 1950s. The Glavins are small farmers, struggling to eke out a living on a poor hill farm. Life is tough, and the characters are preoccupied with trying to provide for themselves. However, change is coming. There is wealth in the country now, and life for men like Mike Glavin is about to change. It does not change quickly enough for Sive, though. She is a victim of her aunt's obsession with money and the security it brings.

The only aspect of *Sive* that is not very representative of the time and place in which the play is set is the idea of a forced match. By the 1950s, such arrangements had all but died out, even in the remotest parts of the country.

Structure of the play

The story of *Sive* is told in a linear fashion. There are no flashbacks and no narration to hint at what is yet to happen. The events unfold over the course of a few weeks. The effect of this is to hold the attention of the audience from start to finish while they watch the conflicts and tensions escalating, and follow the characters as they struggle to either bring about or prevent the match between Sive and Seán Dóta.

Poetry, song and music

Pats Bocock and his son Carthalawn play an important role in *Sive*, commenting on the events of the play, the themes and the characters. In a play where there is no narrator, they are one way for the playwright to let us know his opinion on various matters. They are a unique feature of drama, and part of an old dramatic tradition. In ancient Greek plays, a group of people, called the Chorus, fulfilled the roles that Pats and Carthalawn play in *Sive*.

The travelling men appear at strategic moments in the play, and their arrival lends the events great emotional impact. The rhythm of the bodhrán and the stamping of feet and stick adds to the tension and heightens our awareness of the conflict in each situation.

> The travelling men appear at strategic moments in the play, and their arrival lends the events great emotional impact

THE COMPARATIVE STUDY: **LITERARY GENRE**

The stage directions tell us that Pats and Carthalawn march in step and that all their songs have the same tune. The introduction of the songs is dramatic, all the more so because it is the same each time. The audience soon learns what to expect from the singers, and awaits their commentary and curses with keen interest. Before each song, Pats taps the floor with his stick and calls, 'Carthalawn! Your best! Your mighty best!'

It is Pats and Carthalawn who have the final word in the play. In language reminiscent of an old folk song, Carthalawn laments Sive's death and points the finger of blame very clearly at those who sought to profit from the ill-fated match:

Oh, come all good men and true,
A sad tale I'll tell to you
All of a maiden fair, who died this day;
Oh, they murdered lovely Sive,
She would not be a bride,
And they laid her dead, to bury in the clay.

Stage directions

The stage directions in *Sive* serve a number of different purposes, the first of which is to set the scene. The directions at the start of the play give us a fairly brief but accurate description of an Irish farmhouse of the time. They are precise and authentic. The Glavins' kitchen is primitive. The cooking is done in a skillet hanging over an open fire, and the 'enamel bucket of drinking water' on the table tells us that there is no running water. The family's milk is stored in a creamery tank, and sacks of flour and animal feed are propped against the wall beside it. All of these directions indicate that life in this place is hard, and that there is no money to spare on luxuries. Everything in the kitchen has a purpose. There is no room here for anything or, by implication, anyone idle or useless.

The stage directions also assist in character creation. Before a word is spoken, we have formed an impression of Nanna and Mena and the relationship that exists between them. Nanna is dressed in the traditional costume of an elderly Irish woman of the time: black skirts over red petticoats, and 'long boots tied up to her shins'. We are given the impression that she is a representative of the older generation and of past times. Her body language tells us that she does not have a particular role in this house, and that she is ill at ease and slightly afraid. She has nothing to do but idly stir the fire with the tongs while at the same time 'surreptitiously' smoking a clay pipe. She hastily hides the pipe when Mena enters, which shows that she is wary of the other woman. The words used to describe Mena are an early indication of her personality. There is nothing soft, gentle or particularly feminine about her. She is 'hard-featured' with dark hair tied back so severely that she has 'the appearance of being in want of hair'.

The stage directions continue to inform our opinion of the characters and the relationships between them throughout the play. The increased tension surrounding the match is reflected in the increased hostility in the characters' speech and body language. When Mena and Nanna clash in Act 1, Scene 3, we are told that Mena's voice is 'full of venom' and that she shouts 'violently' at the old woman. She moves aggressively, bouncing towards Nanna until she is close enough to intimidate her, 'stiffening with rage' in reaction to Nanna's jibe about her childlessness, drawing back her hand 'to strike a blow'. Nanna's vulnerability and powerlessness is conveyed equally clearly. She looks at the fire as she speaks, and her voice is 'full of defeat'.

> The increased tension surrounding the match is reflected in the increased hostility in the characters' speech and body language

Dialogue

While dialogue is a feature of each of the three literary genres studied for the Leaving Certificate, its role in drama is more important than it is in novels or films, as it is the main method of storytelling.

The opening lines of dialogue in *Sive* provide us with a great deal of information about the characters, their relationships, the background to the main story, and the themes.

Mena's first words to Nanna are an accusation, and the old woman's

THE COMPARATIVE STUDY: LITERARY GENRE

replies are hostile and defensive. There is no love lost between these two women, and their hate-filled conversation is our first indication of the conflict that pervades the play. The roles of the women in the house are established, as is their unwillingness to concede any respect or authority to the other. Both refer to their shared home as 'my own house'. When Sive enters, Mena instantly goes on the attack, saying that she hopes Sive does not expect her to have a hot dinner ready for her 'any minute of the day you decide to come home'. As Sive has just explained that her bicycle had a double puncture, Mena knows quite well that she did not 'decide' to come home late. Mena's unwelcoming comment shows that she resents and dislikes Sive.

Sive's remarks in the first scene tell us a great deal about her character. Unlike Nanna, she does not rise to Mena's taunting, but maintains her dignity and gentle manner. She tries to placate Mena by assuring her that she doesn't need any dinner as she had a cookery class at the convent: 'We had fricassée with dartois for dessert. It was lovely!' From what we know of Mena already, we are aware that she is unlikely to be familiar with either of these French terms, and that she will resent Sive even more for making the contrast between them so obvious. This is proven to be the case, and Mena sneers at Sive's 'high notions'.

Sive's compliant, sweet nature is revealed in her responses to Mena's harsh criticisms and unfair accusations. However, it is clear from the differences in the way they speak that Sive is no match for the forceful, coarse Mena. Sive's correct grammar shows that she is refined and educated. Mena's speech, on the other hand, reveals her lack of education and refinement. She speaks in the vernacular, peppering her comments with words taken from the Irish or peculiar to her local area, as when she says to Nanna, 'Take out your dirty doodeen of a pipe and close your gob on it, woman.'

> *'Take out your dirty doodeen of a pipe and close your gob on it, woman'*

The dialogue in the opening scene both answers and raises

questions about the characters' backgrounds. We learn that Mena married Nanna's son, and that the farm was poorer than it is now before she came, and that she has little respect for her 'poor amadawn' of a husband. We are also fed snippets of information about Sive's parents, starting with Mena's observation that Sive will 'come to no good either, like the one that went before you!' Nanna's unwillingness to provide Sive with any real details about her birth is intriguing: 'Questions! Questions! Nothing but questions! You were a fine common lump of a baby!'

Symbols and imagery

The use of animal imagery abounds in *Sive*, most of it unflattering. Nanna compares Mena to 'a hungry sow' and in a startlingly powerful and strangely eloquent piece of invective, Pats says to Thomasheen, 'You are the bladder of a pig, the snout of a sow; you are the leavings of a hound, the sting of a wasp.'

This imagery has a dual purpose. It shows that the characters are closely connected to the land, and that the natural world is their sole frame of reference. It also hints that the moral vision of several of the characters is almost non-existent, leaving them no better than animals.

> This imagery has a dual purpose. It shows that the characters are closely connected to the land, and that the natural world is their sole frame of reference

Religious imagery also appears repeatedly in *Sive*. It is used to portray characters like Thomasheen as diabolical. Nanna tells Pats not to mind Thomasheen's rude refusal to shake his hand: 'You are as well off, Pats, without the paw of the devil burning your palm.' In reaction to Thomasheen's hostility and scorn, Carthalawn sings a song in which he wishes that the devil may take 'the hairy creature soon'. A short time later, Nanna calls the matchmaking 'the devil's work'.

THE COMPARATIVE STUDY

General Vision and Viewpoint

Higher Level

Past questions on this mode of comparison have tended to focus on the following:

- *How the general vision and viewpoint of a text is determined by the success or failure of a character in his or her efforts to achieve fulfilment*
- *How the reader's attitude towards a central character can shape the vision and viewpoint*
- *How you came to your understanding of the general vision and viewpoint in your chosen text*
- *The way in which a key moment or moments can influence your understanding of the general vision and viewpoint of a text*
- *How the general vision and viewpoint is shaped by the reader's feeling of optimism or pessimism in reading a text*
- *Your understanding of the general vision and viewpoint in your chosen text*
- *Which aspects of the text shaped your emotional response and helped to construct the general vision and viewpoint*
- *What you enjoyed about the general vision and viewpoint of your chosen text.*

The general vision and viewpoint in *Sive* is bleak and pessimistic. This is a tragic tale of an innocent young girl sacrificed to greed and selfishness. Her suffering throughout the play is for nothing, and she is eventually driven to such despair that she takes her own life. Those who try to help Sive are viciously attacked and their efforts ultimately fail. Evil triumphs over good, and true love does not conquer all. There could hardly be a more negative vision of life than that offered by the plot of *Sive*.

A gloomy atmosphere is established by the time and place in which the play is set. The Glavins live on a remote hill farm in the south of Ireland. Their kitchen is 'poorly furnished'; there is no electricity, no running water and all the cooking is done over an open fire. Even by the standards of the 1950s, this is a primitive household. Nanna Glavin wears the traditional black skirts, red petticoats and boots of an old Irish woman, while Sive's clothes are ill fitting. The family struggles to eke out a living on their boggy land. The impression we get is that life is hard and that any benefits of modern living have passed the Glavins by. They travel everywhere with a pony and cart, and Mike farms without the aid of machinery. Nanna tells Sive that when the doctor who delivered her drove up the road to the house, the old people saw 'the two roundy balls of fire' of his headlamps and believed it was the devil approaching. There is nothing uplifting about the setting of the play. Even the time of year (a 'bitter March evening') is depressing, and this impression deepens as the play progresses.

> The characters in *Sive* present us with an overwhelmingly negative view of human nature and relationships

The characters in *Sive* present us with an overwhelmingly negative view of human nature and relationships. The first conversation in the play is a hate-filled, venomous exchange between Mena and Nanna. The two women detest one another and take every opportunity to deride and taunt each other. Nanna taunts Mena with her childlessness and her poverty, while Mena delights in pointing out that Nanna is old and powerless.

Mena's relationships with her niece and with her husband are equally unhappy. She resents Sive and does not see why the girl should have the chances in life that she never had: 'Out working with a farmer you should be, my girl, instead of getting your head filled with high notions.' Neither does Mena make any secret of her contempt for Mike, telling Nanna that she could have made a far better match for herself than with that 'amadawn', and accusing her husband of being a 'man

THE COMPARATIVE STUDY: GENERAL VISION AND VIEWPOINT

of straw' when he objects to the match between Sive and Seán Dóta.

Thomasheen Seán Rua is a thoroughly despicable character. He has a cynical view of love and is only interested in arranging the match between Sive and Seán Dóta because he will make money from it. He is a lying, manipulative bully who will stop at nothing to get his own way. Together with Mena and Mike, he is responsible for Sive's tragic death.

Mike Glavin's main faults are his greed and his weakness. He is an ineffectual man who commands no respect from the other characters. He is, in a way, even more despicable than Thomasheen in that he knows that what he is doing will cause heartbreak to the niece he is supposed to love like a daughter. When he first hears of the match, Mike opposes it violently: 'No! No! A million thousand times no! It would sleep with me for the rest of my days. It would be like tossing the white flower of the canavaun on to the manure heap.' However, within a short time he is admitting to Mena and Thomasheen that 'the money is a great temptation' and he is nothing like as vociferous in his opposition to the match. Although he continues to have reservations about the impending marriage, Mike never really stands up to Mena and Thomasheen. When Liam begs him to consider Sive's future happiness, Mike throws him out of the house. His greatest betrayal of Sive is never allowing her to learn the contents of Liam's letter.

> *'It would be like tossing the white flower of the canavaun on to the manure heap'*

It is deeply depressing that such immoral, selfish people should have the power in the world of the text. All of the characters mentioned above are products of the society of the time, and that is a damning indictment of rural Ireland in the 1950s. What is most damning, however, is that people like them are the new face of the country. Pats Bocock points out Seán Dóta as one of those who will be 'the new lords of the land. God help the land!' This is a very bleak and pessimistic vision of Ireland's future and it implies that greed, selfishness and a lack of morality will continue to triumph over decency and goodness. This comment on the value system inherent in a newly emerging social order in Ireland seems to imply that John B. Keane was less than hopeful about the future of the country should materialism and greed hold sway.

There are several admirable characters in *Sive*: Sive herself, Liam, Pats and Carthalawn, but no matter how they try, they cannot win the day. The hopelessness of their case becomes ever clearer as the play progresses. Sive begs Mena not to force her to marry Seán Dóta, but her pleas fall on deaf ears. Mena cruelly and cunningly strips Sive of hope and happiness. She tells her that her father abandoned her mother when she fell pregnant and that Sive is nothing more than 'a common bye-child – a bastard!' She isolates Sive from Nanna, thereby removing the support the old woman might offer. Most monstrously of all, Mena lies to Sive about Liam, telling her that he called to wish her well in her marriage and to say that he was emigrating. It would be next to impossible not to empathise with Sive as she cries out in anguish, 'Oh! Liam could never do a thing like that.'

> There are several admirable characters in Sive, but no matter how they try, they cannot win the day

Liam does all he can to rescue Sive from the match, but he cannot prevail on Mike or Mena to change their minds. His language is eloquent and moving in its sincerity when he pleads with them to reconsider: 'Surely if ye know God ye must think of this terrible auction. Ye must know that a day will dawn for all of us when an account must be given.' Mike and Mena respond to Liam's heartfelt appeal to their better nature with fury and the threat of violence. Mena drives him from the house, threatening to cut him with the kitchen knife she is holding.

There is little point in Liam or anyone else asking Mike and Mena to reconsider their choice on moral grounds, because they are well aware that what they are doing is wrong but they are still determined to proceed with the match. They have weighed up the price of good against the price of evil, and have come down firmly on the side of evil. They are willing to destroy Sive's life and sell her to a lecherous old man. Thomasheen is equally alive to the fact that Sive does not want to

THE COMPARATIVE STUDY: **GENERAL VISION AND VIEWPOINT**

marry Seán Dóta and that she is in love with Liam, but he does not care. Thomasheen and Mena show just how lacking in any sort of morality they are when they turn on Nanna, threatening her with destitution and physical harm if she crosses them. When she says that there is 'a hatchery of sin' in the house, she is simply insulted and abused.

Goodness has no power in the play. Kindness, love and virtue are mocked and scorned, and those who try to stand up for what is right are defeated. The aggressive, selfish, amoral bullies have the upper hand.

> Kindness, love and virtue are mocked and scorned, and those who try to stand up for what is right are defeated

The ending of *Sive* is utterly bleak and tragic. All hope has vanished with Sive's death, and not a single character emerges unscathed from the awful events of that final night. Liam is devastated to have lost the girl he loves, while the Glavin family face an appalling future of guilt, blame and sorrow as they struggle to cope with Sive's death.

The reaction of each character to Sive's suicide gives us a final insight into the pessimistic vision and viewpoint of the play. Seán Dóta and Thomasheen sneak away in a cowardly fashion, well aware of the role they have played in Sive's death. It is not likely that either of them will ever find happiness now. Thomasheen will not be paid for the match and will therefore be unable to marry his widow woman. Seán Dóta, who for many years has longed for a young wife, will not have one. Mena's plans have also come to nothing. Instead of earning £200 and ridding herself of Sive and Mena, she now has to live with the knowledge that she drove Sive to her death. Mike is reduced to a barely coherent, babbling wreck who seems unable to cope with the enormity of the situation.

Pats and Carthalawn, in their roles as commentators, speak for the playwright when they summarise the recent happenings in a mournful song:

> Oh, they murdered lovely Sive,
> She would not be a bride,
> And they laid her for to bury in the clay.

The final image we are left with is that of the heartbroken Nanna, alone in the room and weeping silently over the body of her dead granddaughter. The tragedy of Sive's death and the triumph of evil and hatred over goodness and love is a deeply pessimistic vision of life.

The imagery in *Sive* contributes greatly to our understanding of the general vision and viewpoint. Similes and metaphors pepper the text and are invariably drawn from nature or religion. This effectively underscores the importance of both of these areas in the lives of the characters. For the most part, the imagery serves to show us that this is a world in which evil is ever-present and in which people give into their baser instincts, thus becoming reduced to a moral state little better than that of animals.

The negative vision of relationships is powerfully conveyed through images of nature. Thomasheen says that women are like giddy heifers or horses and need to be whipped and kept in check. He asks Mena if Sive has agreed to the match with Seán Dóta and claims that he 'will not rest happy till he has the halter on her'. Nanna complains to Mike that Sive is 'for sale like an animal', showing that Mike, Mena and Thomasheen believe a monetary value can be placed on human life and happiness. Relationships are portrayed as little more than bargains and the defeat of the weaker by the stronger. This is a grim vision indeed.

> Relationships are portrayed as little more than bargains and the defeat of the weaker by the stronger

The only person who is described favourably in natural imagery is Sive. Mike says that to marry her to Seán Dóta would be 'like tossing the white flower of the canavaun on to the manure heap', while Liam tells Mike and Mena that Sive is spoken of locally as 'the flower of the parish'. This imagery, which emphasises Sive's beauty and innocence, heightens the impression that she is a delicate creature being abused and mistreated by people who have no respect for the qualities she possesses. The overall impression created by such imagery is dark and pessimistic.

THE COMPARATIVE STUDY

Cultural Context
Higher Level

Social Setting
Ordinary Level

Past questions on these modes of comparison have tended to focus on the following:

Higher Level
- *The way in which the world or culture the characters inhabit affects the storyline*
- *The way in which the world or culture they inhabit shapes the characters' attitudes and values*
- *What is interesting about the world or culture of the texts*
- *How the author establishes the cultural context.*

Ordinary Level
- *What you liked or disliked about the social setting*
- *What you found interesting about the social setting*
- *The way in which the social setting influences the characters*
- *How a key moment can show us the way in which the social setting affects the characters.*

Setting

Sive is set in a remote, hilly farm in the south of Ireland. Life in the Glavin house is primitive, as is expressed in the stage directions. The kitchen is 'poorly furnished', cooking is done over an open fire, and there is no running water. This is clearly a difficult place in which to survive, and this is reflected in the hardness of characters such as Mena and Thomasheen.

The farm is quite isolated: Sive has to walk some distance down the road to borrow a rail from a neighbour, and Thomasheen makes reference to taking a short cut home 'across the mountain'. This isolation makes it easier for Mena to cut Sive off from contact with others in the weeks leading up to the wedding, thus breaking her spirit and bending her more easily to Mena's will.

Religion

Religion does not play a particularly large role in *Sive*, but it does shape the attitudes of the characters to various events in the play. Sive's illegitimacy is a source of shame and is one of the ways Mena and Thomasheen plan to browbeat her into accepting the match with Seán Dóta. Thomasheen says that Mena should tell Sive that she will humiliate her publicly for being 'a bye-child' if the girl does not agree to their proposal. Later, Mena brings up the topic again when trying to persuade Mike that Sive is lucky to get any offer of marriage: 'The child was born in want of wedlock. That much is well known from one end of the parish to the other … What better can she do? Who will take her with the slur and the doubt hanging over her?'

> Sive's illegitimacy is a source of shame and is one of the ways Mena and Thomasheen plan to browbeat her into accepting the match with Seán Dóta

Liam appeals to Mike and Mena to realise that 'a day will dawn for all of us when an account must be given' and begs them not to go ahead with what he calls the 'terrible auction' of Sive to Seán Dóta. In an impassioned speech, he asks if they are 'forgetting Him who died on Calvary' and compares their treatment of Sive to pushing 'hard crooked thorns deep into His helpless body'. When they ignore his entreaties, Liam reflects that 'nothing in Heaven or Hell could move ye to see wrong!' Mike and Mena may pay lip service to religion, but it does not affect their moral decision making. They are not alone in this. When Thomasheen is telling Mike and Mena about his late father, he prefaces the story with 'God rest him', yet moments later goes on to denounce the dead man as 'an amadawn, a stump of a fool who took his life by his own hand'. The speech of the characters in *Sive* may be peppered with references to God, heaven and hell, but there is little real religious feeling behind most of it. An exception to this is Liam Scuab, who possesses religious sensibilities and moral vision in equal measure. At the end of the play, when he carries Sive's body into the house, Liam curses Mena and wishes that 'the hand of Jesus may strike you dead where you stand'. His words carry power because we know that he is on the side of goodness and right.

Mike is horrified that Sive's suicide will mean that she cannot be 'buried in holy ground'. (At the time, the Catholic Church refused proper funeral rites and burial in church cemeteries to those who had taken their own life.) He babbles idiotically about the need to go for a priest, but when Liam tells him to go and get one, he says there is 'no luck in going for a priest alone'. This blend of religion and superstition runs throughout the play. Pats Bocock and Carthalawn use their songs to curse those who cross them in a tradition that has more to do with pre-Christian Ireland than Christianity, but they also tell Nanna that 'we do be praying for you in our prayers, whenever we get the notion to kneel'. Thomasheen advises against Sive walking down the road alone as he claims that 'there is no telling what you would meet on a black road', and warning her about 'the phuca' with the 'mad red eyes on him like coals of fire lighting in his head'.

Money

Money is hugely important in *Sive*. It is because of money that Thomasheen and Mena resolve to make the match between Sive and Seán Dóta; a decision which ultimately leads to Sive's untimely death. To be without money is to be without power or independence in the world of the play. Mena cannot shake off the memories of her poor upbringing when she and her sisters would 'sit into the night talking and thieving and wondering where the next ha'penny would come from'. Nanna mocks Mena's family's poverty, saying that they used to drink their tea 'out of jam pots for the want of cups'.

When Mike returns home from the market, Mena immediately asks him how much he made, and when he does not reply straight away, repeats the question. She is satisfied with the amount earned but is determined to be frugal with it: 'We will mind whatever penny we make.'

Mike is as fond of money as his wife is. He is pleased that the lot of small farmers is improving and he likes the fact that the shopkeepers are now treating them with some respect: 'It does the heart good to see the shopkeepers scrapin' and bowin'.' He tells Mena that 'money is the best friend a man ever had'.

Thomasheen is also driven by the need to amass wealth for himself. He has his eye on a local widow and believes that the money he makes from the match between Sive and Seán Dóta will allow him to marry her. He had a similar chance many years ago, but lost the woman he wanted because his father committed suicide and Thomasheen had to spend all his money on the funeral.

> *'money is the best friend a man ever had'*

For Mena, Mike and Thomasheen, money represents independence and the chance of a better life. Anyone who has money need never be ashamed or beholden to shopkeepers and others. All of them have known poverty and all are determined to better their lives if at all possible. It is hardly surprising, given this, that Mena and Thomasheen leap on the chance to marry Sive to Seán Dóta in exchange for quite a considerable sum of money. Mike is dead set against the match when he first hears of it, voicing his disgust, 'A million thousand times no!', and vowing that he will never agree to such a thing. However, it is not long before he begins to change his tune, admitting to Mena that 'the money is a great temptation'. Eventually he allows himself to be completely corrupted by the thought of the £200 and by the pressure of his wife and Thomasheen. In many ways, Mike's betrayal of Sive is worse than Mena or Thomasheen's behaviour because he genuinely cares for Sive, unlike the other two. It is a mark of his greed that he consents to the match, albeit with misgivings.

Money does not have the hold over Sive and Liam that it does over the older characters in the play. The young lovers are part of a different generation, and view life differently. Thus, when Mena tries to persuade Sive of the benefits of marrying Seán Dóta, her arguments fall on deaf ears. Mena begs Sive to 'thank God that you won't be for the rest of your days working for the bare bite and the sup like the poor women of these parts', but Sive is concerned only with the revulsion she feels for Seán Dóta and the impossibility of someone of her age marrying such an old man: 'Imagine what the girls at school would say! Imagine going to a dance with him, or going to chapel with him!' Mena has always viewed marriage as a bargain, but Sive and Liam could never marry for money, only for love.

> Seán Dóta is rich by the standards of the day, and this is enough to make him a suitable match in Mena's eyes

Seán Dóta is rich by the standards of the day, and this is enough to make him a suitable match in Mena's eyes. John B. Keane ensures that there is nothing even remotely attractive about the man: he is old, 'wizened', uneducated, lecherous, and possessed of irritating mannerisms such as his 'half laugh' whenever he speaks. Seán Dóta is the antithesis of the handsome, refined, intelligent Liam Scuab. However, Mena and Mike consider the older man the better catch because he has 'the grass of twenty cows' and 'the holding of money'.

Mike, Mena and Thomasheen are so corrupted by greed that they are willing to sacrifice Sive's happiness for a couple of hundred pounds. Liam calls what they are doing 'a terrible auction' and Nanna tells Mike that she cannot stand by and watch her granddaughter offered up 'for sale like an animal'. Their pleas to Mena and Mike to reconsider their actions come to nothing, as they are consumed by the thought of the money.

In *Sive* we are presented with a world in which greed holds sway and in which money is considered more important than anything, even love and happiness.

Power

Power in *Sive* is equated with having money. Seán Dóta is effectively able to 'buy' Sive because she is a young girl without any fortune of her own. Mena points out to Sive that if she marries the old man she will have money too and will be independent: 'You will have no enemy when you have the name of money.' She attempts to win the girl over by saying that when she is rich she will be in a superior position to all her neighbours and will be able to drive past them with her 'head in the air'. Cynically, Thomasheen advises Mena to tell Sive that she would do well to marry Seán Dóta as he is likely to die soon, leaving her a wealthy widow who will then be in a position to 'pick and choose from the bucks of the parish'. To Mena and Thomasheen, the situation is clear. Sive would be most foolish to turn down this chance to make her fortune and, in so doing, raise herself up from her current, powerless state as a young, penniless, illegitimate orphan.

> *'You will have no enemy when you have the name of money'*

The Ireland of the play is changing. Those who were previously poor and powerless, small farmers like Mike, are now coming into their own. Mike is delighted to see the increase in prices for his livestock at the market, and shopkeepers showing him respect for the first time. He remarks to Mena that 'the boot is on the other foot now' and tells her that it 'does the heart good to see the shopkeepers scrapin' and bowin''.

Mike is not the only one to have noticed this shift in the balance of power. Pats Bocock says, 'There is money-making everywhere. The face of the country is changing. The small man with the one cow and the pig and the bit of bog is coming into his own.' This change does not seem to appeal to Pats, who wonders how farmers will cope with their new role: 'What way will he rule? What way will he hould up under the new riches?' The evidence from *Sive* would seem to indicate that the newly rich will be corrupted by their wealth. Pats is not confident that the new Ireland will be a better one. He points at Seán Dóta as he says: 'The likes of him will be the new lords of the land. God help the land!'

The way Mena, Thomasheen and Seán Dóta treat Pats and

THE COMPARATIVE STUDY: CULTURAL CONTEXT • SOCIAL SETTING

Carthalawn is another indication of the change in Irish life. In past times, the travelling men had power and were respected and welcomed wherever they went. Their bringing of news, storytelling, poetry and song was appreciated and rewarded. Now it is only Nanna and Mike who show them any sort of hospitality when they visit. Thomasheen treats them with contempt, jeeringly calling them 'the two biggest robbers walking the roads of Ireland' and telling them to stop 'disgustin' respectable people'. Of course, Thomasheen is far less respectable than either Pats or his son, but because he is better off than they are, he sees himself as superior.

Pats and Carthalawn, like Liam and Nanna, have a moral power. They represent qualities such as honesty, love, decency and integrity. However, Mena and Thomasheen sneer at such qualities, and view them as weak. Thomasheen cannot understand Liam's genuine love for Sive and is scornful of the romantic sentiments the young man expresses in the letter he tries to have secretly delivered to the girl. Thomasheen believes that a man should exert his power over a woman more forcefully, and should not try to woo her this way. He tells Mike that Liam will 'never have a woman the way he is going about it' and says the young man should know that courting a girl is simply 'the ketchin' of a hoult until she is winded. That's the time for words with a woman.'

> Pats and Carthalawn, like Liam and Nanna, have a moral power. They represent qualities such as honesty, love, decency and integrity

The bleak message in *Sive* is that moral power is not enough to win the day. Liam, Pats and Carthalawn fail in their attempt to rescue Sive, and Nanna is unable to persuade Mike that the match should not go ahead. Sive is powerless to choose whom she wants to marry and feels that the only option left to her is to take her own life. The final image in the play, of Nanna weeping silently over the body of her dead granddaughter, is a poignant reminder of the fact that decency, love and integrity are not enough to win the day.

Gender

The world of *Sive* is largely male-dominated. The men own the land

and control the money. The older generation of men will only consider marrying a woman if she brings money of her own to the match. Mike is astonished when Mena tells him that a wealthy farmer wants to marry Sive: 'What farmer of that size would take her without money?' Mena herself had to work for her 'fortune' and bemoans the fact that she didn't wait longer and make a better match for herself. She also begrudges Sive her second-level education, saying that when she was Sive's age she 'worked from dawn to dark to put aside my fortune'.

Because they do not have any real power, the women in the text must turn to other means to get their way. Thomasheen advises Mena to use her sexual wiles to win Mike over to the idea of the match: 'Aren't ye in the one bed sleeping? Ye will have yeer own talk. You will come around him aisy.' Nanna uses her status as Mike's mother to try to win him round: 'Surely you will listen to your own mother that loved you as no one ever will.' Sive does not have Mena or Nanna's determination and feisty spirit, so she is completely powerless. When Mike finds her talking to Liam in the kitchen, he sends her to her room and tells Liam he cannot see her again. When we think that Sive is a young woman of around eighteen years of age who must obey her uncle's wishes and is not free to marry the man of her choice, we appreciate how patriarchal the society of the text is. However, it must be noted that even in 1950s Ireland the idea of forced marriages and matchmaking was outdated. This is the reason that the match between Sive and Seán Dóta is such a talking point among the locals. Liam tells Mike and Mena that 'the public houses are full with the mockery of it'.

> Because they do not have any real power, the women in the text must turn to other means to get their way

Marriage and love

There are two attitudes to love and marriage in this play. One is that marriage is nothing but a business transaction, while the other is that it is a union of two people who love one another very much.

The only married couple we meet in the play are Mike and Mena.

THE COMPARATIVE STUDY: **CULTURAL CONTEXT • SOCIAL SETTING**

Their marriage does not appear to be a loving one at all. Mena speaks scornfully to and about Mike. She tells Nanna that she could have made a better match for herself than with her 'poor amadawn of a son', and calls Mike a 'man of straw' when he objects to the match between Sive and Thomasheen. Mena makes no secret of the fact that she sees marriage as nothing more or less than a business arrangement. She grew up in a desperately poor household where she and her sisters longed for the chance to marry and thus escape their harsh life. She tells Sive: 'We would fire embers of fire at the devil to leave the misery of our own house before us, to make a home with a man, any man that would show us four walls for his time in the world.' It is hardly surprising, given her background, that Mena thinks Sive should consider herself lucky to have the opportunity to marry a wealthy man like Seán Dóta. She stresses the material advantages of the match when trying to persuade Sive to agree to it: 'Think of the handling of thousands and the fine clothes and the perfumery. Think of the hundreds of pounds in creamery cheques that will come in the door to you and the servant boy and the servant girl falling all over you for fear you might dirty your hands with work.'

> Mena makes no secret of the fact that she sees marriage as nothing more or less than a business arrangement

Thomasheen has a similarly pragmatic approach to relationships. He admits that he did love a girl once, but that he was not able to marry the girl because he had to spend all his money on his father's funeral. Perhaps embittered by this experience, Thomasheen now scorns love. He tells Mike and Mena that it is not for people like them and mocks the romantic sentiments Liam Scuab expresses in his letter to Sive: 'He will never have a woman the way he is going about it!' Yet, for all that he derides Liam's romantic nature, Thomasheen shows a curious understanding of loving relationships. When he is asking Mena if Mike has ever spoken 'the word of love' to her, he waxes lyrical in his own way. 'Did he run to you when he come in from the bog and put his arms around you and give you a big smohawnach of a kiss and tell you that the length of the day was like the length of a million years when he was separated from you?' Even though he is being cynical, Thomasheen clearly knows how a loving couple should behave. On another occasion he admits to Mena that he is lonely: 'I am a single man. I know what a man have to do who have no woman to lie with him. He have to drink hard, or he have to walk under the black sky when every eye is closed in sleep.'

Like Thomasheen, Mike knows what romance is, even if it is not a feature of his own marriage. He is unhappy with the match between Sive and Seán Dóta because he knows that she does not love him: 'Sive is young, with a brain by her. She will be dreaming about love with a young man. 'Tis the way young girls do be!'

Mena, Mike and Thomasheen are products of an upbringing marked by poverty and by the need to make a good match in order to have any hope of a better life. In this context, their behaviour might be understood, even though it cannot be approved of.

Liam Scuab and Sive are representatives of a new generation of Irish people. They are appalled at the idea of matchmaking and cannot imagine marrying someone they do not love. Nanna tells Mike that 'there is a sweet thing in their love'. Unlike Mike and Mena, Liam does not see Sive's illegitimacy as an obstacle to their marriage. While Mena believes that nobody decent would take 'a bye-child' like Sive 'with the slur and the doubt hanging over her', Liam repeatedly expresses his desire to marry her.

> *'She will be dreaming about love with a young man. 'Tis the way young girls do be!'*

THE COMPARATIVE STUDY

Theme or Issue

Higher Level and Ordinary Level

Past questions on this mode of comparison have tended to focus on the following:

Higher Level
- *What insights you gained from studying the theme*
- *How the study of a particular text changed or reinforced your view of the theme*
- *The way in which key moments can heighten your awareness of a particular theme*
- *How the presentation of the theme can add to the impact of the text*
- *How the theme helps to maintain your interest in the text.*

Ordinary Level
- *What you learned about your chosen theme*
- *How a key moment in the text reveals the theme*
- *Why you feel that the theme made the text interesting*
- *How the theme is presented in the text*
- *How the theme plays an important role in the story*
- *How the theme affects the life of a character in the text.*

Theme 1: escape

Escape is a central theme of *Sive*. The central character Sive obviously strives to escape the vile match which has been arranged for her, but she is not the only one who longs to break free.

Mena is damaged and embittered by her poverty-stricken upbringing. She grew up in a house where she and her sisters 'would fire embers of fire at the devil to leave the misery of our own house behind us, to make a home with a man, any man that would show four walls to us for his time in the world'. She marries Mike to escape this dreadful life, but she cannot shake off her past life, no matter how much she may want to. Nanna is partly to blame for this. She jeers at Mena's poor upbringing, claiming that her father was 'a half starved bocock of a beggar' and that Mena and her family used to drink 'tay out of jam pots for the want of cups'.

Mena's inability to leave her past behind contributes to her resentment of Sive. When Mena was young, she had to earn her dowry so that she could marry: 'When I was her age in my father's house I worked from dawn till dark to put aside my fortune.' Sive does not have to do this as her mother asked on her death bed that Sive be educated, and Mike honours his promise to see to Sive's schooling.

> her mother asked on her death bed that Sive be educated, and Mike honours his promise to see to Sive's schooling

Her impoverished childhood makes Mena view marriage simply as a means to an end.

She is probably quite sincere when she says that Sive will do well to marry Seán Dóta: 'Will you thank God that you won't be for the rest of your days working for the bare bite and sup like the poor women of these parts.' Mena cannot understand that Sive is appalled at the thought of marrying for money. To Mena, this would have been an ideal situation. Her marriage to Mike has been unsatisfactory in that she still has to 'mind whatever penny we make'.

Mena's character is not an admirable one, mainly because of her greed and her hardness. Yet if we look closely at the description she gives of her early life, perhaps we can gain a greater understanding of part of her eagerness to arrange the match. Mena fears poverty. She longs to be independent and she believes she is offering good advice to Sive when she says: 'You will have no enemy when you have the name of money.' Of course, it is not just Sive's future Mena is talking about here. If the match goes ahead, Mena will be paid £200. She will also be independent and will at last be able to break free from the grip of poverty.

THE COMPARATIVE STUDY: **THEME OR ISSUE**

Mike, too, is greatly influenced by his past. He cannot escape the memory of his dead sister, and is terrified that Sive will end up in the same situation. His inability to move on from the events surrounding Sive's birth mean that Mike does not behave rationally or kindly when he discovers the relationship between Liam Scuab and Sive. It was Liam's cousin who fathered Sive, and Mike wrongly believes that he abandoned her when she was pregnant. Liam tries to tell him that this was not the case: 'You know as well as I do that he would have married her. You know he went across to England to make a home for her but he was drowned. He never knew she was with child when he left.' Liam's language (the repetition of 'You know') implies that Mike has been told this story before, but he still refuses to believe it, clinging stubbornly to his own version of past events. He cannot shake off the notion that Liam is the same as his cousin and that he will take advantage of Sive. He dismisses Liam's explanation as 'quick words', and throws him out of the house. Mike has made the past a prison for some of his darkest thoughts and he is oddly unwilling to free himself, even when presented with the means to do so.

> 'You know he went across to England to make a home for her but he was drowned'

The setting of the play (all the action takes place in one room) adds to the idea that Sive and the other characters are trapped. The farm itself is in a remote, hilly spot and the nearest neighbours are some distance away. The rather claustrophobic atmosphere of the Glavins' kitchen deepens, and as the play progresses it becomes more and more apparent that Sive has no hope of getting away.

From the moment the idea of a match between Sive and Seán Dóta is made known to the girl, she is desperate to avoid such a dreadful fate. She loathes the lecherous little man and is appalled when he makes a pass at her on the dark road, telling Nanna in disgust that he is 'like an ould sick thing'. She is determined not to have anything to do with Seán Dóta and tells Mena: 'I could never live with that old man.' However, the audience is privy to knowledge that Sive is not. We know that Mena is determined that the match shall go ahead as she is highly motivated by the thought of earning £200 if her niece agrees to marry Seán Dóta. Mena is such a strong character, and she and Thomasheen are such a diabolically cunning and manipulative team, that we fear Sive may be unable to avoid acquiescing to their plan.

Sive has allies in Nanna, Liam, Pats Bocock and Carthalawn. They are all united in their determination to rescue Sive from the match, but they are not as powerful as Mena and Thomasheen. The latter pair contrive to cut off all of Sive's means of escape, and methodically set about doing so.

Mena's plan is twofold. She will remove all hope from Sive's life, and will manipulate her into believing that the only option left to her is to marry Seán Dóta. At the same time, she ensures that Sive cannot physically leave the house or even her bedroom without Mena knowing.

The first stage in breaking Sive's spirit, and thus making her too defeated and unhappy to even try to get away, is telling her that she is illegitimate. Sive has always wanted to know about her parents, and Mena pretends to be on her side: 'I will tell the tale. Himself would never bring himself to say it.' She also claims that Nanna will not tell Sive the truth. Of course, it is Mena who lies, telling Sive that her father 'disappeared like the mist of a May morning', abandoning her mother when she fell pregnant. When Sive does not appear sufficiently distressed by this tale, Mena harshly tells her: 'You are a bye-child, a common bye-child – a bastard.' Sive attempts to leave the room, but Mena even cuts off this avenue of escape, forcing Sive back into the chair and making her listen to what she has to say. She informs Sive that she will no longer be leaving the house to go to school, and that she can no longer share a room with Nanna. From now on, Sive will sleep in a room which is accessed through Mena's own room.

> Sive attempts to leave the room, but Mena even cuts off this avenue of escape, forcing Sive back into the chair

Sive's new bedroom being behind Mena's room is a metaphor for Mena ensuring that everyone who wishes to get to Sive from now on

THE COMPARATIVE STUDY: **THEME OR ISSUE**

will have to go through her. She stands between Sive and any possible means of escape. This is seen clearly when she prevents Liam from speaking to Sive when he calls. She has Mike on her side in this; he also tells Liam that he cannot see Sive: 'She's in my care. You'll have to talk with me.' Liam is forced to leave without meeting Sive, but she emerges from her room after he has gone, claiming she heard his voice. Now Mena shows just how cruel she can be. Feigning innocence, she proceeds to break Sive's heart and her spirit by telling her that Liam called to wish her well in her marriage and to say that he is leaving the area for good. A defeated Sive flees to her room in tears, believing at last that there is no hope for her and that nothing can save her now. It appears that Mena has finally succeeded in forcing Sive down the path she has chosen for her.

> A defeated Sive flees to her room in tears, believing at last that there is no hope for her and that nothing can save her now

This is a bleak moment in the play, but hope of escape appears in the form of Pats Bocock. The night before the wedding he manages to deliver a letter to Nanna which contains plans for Sive to sneak out of the window of her room when everyone is asleep, and go to Liam's house. He will be waiting for her and they will drive straight to the city to get married. The gloomy atmosphere is lifted, and we believe that Sive may yet get away to be with the man she loves. This hope is soon crushed, however, when Thomasheen intercepts the letter and destroys it. Sive never learns of the plan.

Sive does manage to escape that night, but not to run to the young man she loves. Poignantly, she leaves through her bedroom window, just as Liam had proposed in his plan, but instead of running to the man she loves, she runs across the bog and to her death.

With Sive's death Mike and Mena's hopes of escape also die. Mena will never get the money and the security she wants and will continue to live in fear of poverty. Mike now has another death to haunt him for the rest of his life, but this one promises to trouble his conscience far more than his sister's ever did. Mike played no part in his sister's end, but he cannot escape the knowledge that he bears great responsibility for Sive's death. When he first heard of the proposed match, he told Mena that he could not agree to it as such a thing would 'sleep with me for the rest of my days'. We can be sure that his part in Sive's death will affect him far more deeply than his part in the match ever could have.

Theme 2: conflict

The idea of conflict is introduced at the very beginning of *Sive*. Even before a word is spoken, the stage directions tell us that Nanna is 'surreptitiously smoking a clay pipe'. The word 'surreptitiously' tells us that Nanna is ill at ease and concerned lest she be caught. Sure enough, when she hears the door opening, Nanna hastily conceals the pipe in her skirts.

Mena's first words bear out our initial impression that there is tension in this household. She suspects that Nanna has been smoking, though the old woman denies it. The conversation that follows is full of hostility and it is not long before what began as a relatively minor matter, Nanna hiding her pipe, becomes an emotionally charged, abusive encounter in which Nanna berates Mena for her childlessness, and Mena claims that she could have made a far better match for herself than with Nanna's 'poor amadawn of a son', Mike.

The root of the conflict between these two women is their relative positions in the household. Nanna should defer to Mena as the new head of the house, but is unwilling to do so. She asks crossly if she is 'to be scolded night and day in my own house' and later tells Mena, 'I was here before you.' Mena, for her part, is equally unwilling to treat Nanna with the respect due to an elderly mother-in-law.

Another source of conflict in the Glavin family is Sive. Mena is jealous of the preferential treatment her niece receives, and does not see why the girl should be at school instead of 'out working with a farmer' the way Mena was at her age. She also taunts Sive with her illegitimacy,

THE COMPARATIVE STUDY: **THEME OR ISSUE**

telling her that she will 'come to no good either, like the one that went before you'.

Although Sive, unlike Nanna, does not deliberately provoke Mena to anger, her behaviour nonetheless infuriates her aunt. When Sive arrives home from school late and Mena tells her that she cannot expect to have dinner waiting for her whenever she turns up, Sive politely and eagerly attempts to reassure Mena that there is no need for an evening meal by saying that she had 'a cookery class at the convent today, all the girls had dinner there. We had fricassée with dartois for dessert'. Mena is openly scornful of what she considers to be Sive's 'high notions' and it seems clear that nothing the girl does will please her critical, envious aunt.

Sive's birth gives rise to conflict in the text. The attitude towards unmarried mothers is negative, and Mena uses the girl's illegitimacy as a way to goad her and Nanna, saying that Sive will 'come to no good either, like the one who went before'. Thomasheen and Mena both seize on this conflict to force Sive to marry Seán Dóta. Mena tells Mike that nobody else is likely to marry Sive 'with the slur and the doubt hanging over her', and she harshly tells Sive that she is 'a common bye-child – a bastard' in an effort to break her spirit. Mike is afraid that Sive will also become pregnant out of wedlock, a fact Thomasheen latches on to. He warns Mike that Liam Scuab and Sive are meeting secretly, and Mike is very alarmed: 'This is more serious than I thought and 'twill have to stop! I don't want her going the same road as her mother.'

> *"twill have to stop! I don't want her going the same road as her mother"*

Sive's relationship with Liam Scuab also causes conflict in the Glavin house. Mike does not want the pair to see each other at all as he blames Liam's cousin for fathering Sive and abandoning her mother, Mike's sister. Liam protests that his cousin went to England to set up a home there for Sive's mother but was drowned before he could do so. Mike will hear no word of explanation from Liam and goes so far as to threaten Liam's life, warning darkly that the young man 'will pay as dear as your cousin paid, maybe'.

Nanna supports the young couple, discreetly leaving them alone together when Liam calls unexpectedly. Her defence of Liam places Nanna in a position of conflict with her own son and adds to the lack of harmony in the household.

It is Thomasheen Seán Rua who sparks off the battle of wills in the Glavin family that exacerbates the tensions in the relationships between the family members and eventually leads to Sive taking her own life. He is a powerful, destructive force in the text and is fiendishly manipulative and ruthless. He is determined to arrange the wholly inappropriate match between Sive and the elderly, lecherous Seán Dóta and will stop at nothing to achieve his aim. It is in Thomasheen's interest to encourage Mena's hatred of her niece and mother-in-law. He says sympathetically that he often wonders how Mena puts up with all she has to endure from the pair, and points out that if the match goes ahead, Mena will be rid of Nanna as well as Sive. He advises Mena to threaten Sive with public humiliation if she refuses to marry Seán Dóta, and warns against allowing Nanna to interfere with their plans.

> He is a powerful, destructive force in the text and is fiendishly manipulative and ruthless

The proposed match appals Mike and he initially refuses to countenance it. Mena is enraged by his claim that Sive is too young and too romantic to be forced into an arranged marriage. Her bitterness at having to marry Mike in order to escape the poverty of her family home comes to the fore, and she scornfully accuses her husband of being 'a man of straw'. Husband and wife fight bitterly and Mike eventually storms out of the kitchen in a violent rage, with Mena hot on his heels.

The conflict in the Glavin household intensifies as the play progresses. Those who oppose the match and those who support it become ever more desperate to achieve their aims. Verbal threats are backed up with physical threats. Mena and Thomasheen round on Nanna when they have her alone and threaten her with destitution if she stands in their way. Mena moves to strike her, saying, 'I will take

THE COMPARATIVE STUDY: **THEME OR ISSUE**

the head from your shoulders,' but she is held back by Thomasheen. Liam is met with an equally violent response when he speaks out against the match. Mike tells him to 'get out of this house before I be tempted to take a weapon in my hands'. Mena is even more aggressive and threatening, saying first that she will burn him with the fire tongs and then, when Liam begs her to see that what she is doing to Sive is sinful, snatching a knife and shouting: 'I'll open you! I'll open you if you vex me more.' It is clear that in this conflict between good and evil, evil is more powerful.

> *'I'll open you! I'll open you if you vex me more'*

The victim of all of this conflict and hatred is Sive. She has done nothing to deserve it, but she is abused and badly treated by her warring family and by the greedy and amoral Thomasheen. Her death brings an end to the immediate conflict, but it will undoubtedly be a further source of bitter conflict between Mike, Mena and Nanna. It is impossible to imagine them ever resolving their differences after the tragic event.

THE COMPARATIVE STUDY

Relationships

Ordinary Level **or** as a **Theme Option** for Higher Level

Past questions on Relationships (Ordinary Level) have tended to focus on the following:
- *Why you find the relationship to be complicated*
- *Why you consider the relationship to be successful*
- *Why you consider the relationship to be a failure*
- *Why the relationship made a strong impression on you.*

Mena and Nanna

The relationship between Mena and Nanna is a tense, poisonous one. They do not have a good word to say to or about one another at any stage in the play.

The situation in the Glavin household, in which daughter-in-law and mother-in-law live together, was not uncommon in Ireland at the time the play was written. The arrangement could work well on occasion, but it often led to a strained relationship between the two women, both of whom felt they were in charge of the household. This is certainly the case in *Sive*, and the power struggle between wife and mother-in-law is obvious from the outset. When Mena complains about Nanna hiding her pipe, Nanna responds: 'Am I to be scolded, night and day, in my own house?' A short time later, Mena reacts angrily to Nanna cursing her 'in my own house'. Nanna's response, 'I was here before you', is met with a venomous and triumphant, 'Ah, but you won't be here after me!' from Mena.

Both women are at fault in this case. Nanna should defer to Mena as the new head of the household, while Mena should treat Nanna with the respect due to her age and position in the family. Neither woman is prepared to make these concessions, and the resulting acrimony causes great unhappiness in the Glavin home.

Part of the problem in the relationship between Nanna and Mena is that they are quite similar in some ways. Neither can hold her tongue, and both are quick to fly into a temper and lash out with a cruel insult or threat. The stage directions add to the impression that this relationship is a dreadful one. The women speak to one another 'harshly', 'irritably', 'crossly' and 'viciously'.

There is occasionally humour in these exchanges between the two women, such as when Mena warns Nanna that if she continues to hide her pipe under her skirts it will eventually catch fire and Nanna will 'go off in a big ball of smoke and ashes'. Nanna's response, 'If I do, 'tis my prayer that the wind will blow me in your direction and I'll have the satisfaction of taking you with me', is highly entertaining. Of course, it is only the audience who enjoy the humorous aspects of the women's bickering; Nanna and Mena are deadly serious when they hurl such venomous comments at one another.

Another source of conflict between Mena and Nanna is the issue of Mena's childlessness. If there were children in the house, Nanna's role would be clearer in that she would be expected to help rear them while Mena worked in the house and on the farm. Nanna uses Mena's infertility as a weapon in their hate-filled exchanges: 'Aha, you'd burn well, for you're as dry as the hobs of hell inside you. Every woman of your age in the parish has a child of her own and nothing to show by you.' Mena is equally scathing and unkind about what she sees as Nanna's lack of contribution to the running of the house, accusing her of being a useless burden on the family.

> *'Every woman of your age in the parish has a child of her own and nothing to show by you'*

The terrible relationship between Nanna and Mena affects everyone in the Glavin household. Mike is made miserable by being torn between his mother and his wife, both of whom appeal to him to take their side when it comes to the match between Sive and Seán Dóta.

THE COMPARATIVE STUDY: **RELATIONSHIPS**

Sive also suffers as a result of the two women's hatred for one another. Part of the reason Mena is so keen to arrange the match is that Seán Dóta is willing to take Nanna to live with Sive in her new home. Mena is delighted at this prospect, telling Thomasheen: 'I would give my right hand to have that oul' hag out of my way.'

Unwittingly, Sive herself contributes to the friction between Nanna and Mena. Mena resents what she sees as the preferential treatment Sive receives: 'Why should that young rip be sent to a convent every day instead of being out working with a farmer?' That Nanna should tax Mena with her childlessness while at the same time showering affection on her illegitimate granddaughter is difficult for Mena to bear and adds to her dislike of Nanna. She complains to Thomasheen that Sive and Nanna are 'as thick as thieves' and suspects them of conspiring against her.

> *'I would give my right hand to have that oul' hag out of my way'*

Thomasheen is a master of manipulation, and he seizes on the animosity between Mena and Nanna, using it to further his own interests. He tells Mena that if she agrees to the match she will be 'rid of the old woman too'. He says he will make it part of the bargain that Nanna goes to live with Sive and Seán Dóta, and sympathises with Mena's situation: 'I often wonder how you put up with it all.' Thomasheen deliberately fuels Mena's hatred of Nanna and warns her that the old woman may thwart their plans for the match if not kept in her place.

The moment of greatest tension in the relationship between Nanna and Mena comes when Nanna tackles Mena and Thomasheen about the proposed match, calling it 'the devil's work'. Mena rounds viciously on the old woman as soon as she and Thomasheen have her alone, telling her that she is 'a lone woman with your husband feeding worms in the trench'. She goes on to threaten to throw Nanna out of the house, and mocks her scornfully for being like 'a child in the cot feeding yourself up with the fruits of our labours'. Nanna picks up on this reference to a child in the cradle and taunts Mena with it. Enraged beyond measure, Mena goes to strike Nanna: 'I will take the head from your shoulders.' She is only prevented from doing so by Thomasheen. The animosity between the two women has now escalated to the point where physical violence threatens to replace verbal hostility. Nanna leaves, saying as she does so that there is 'a hatchery of sin in this house'. The full extent of the women's loathing for one another has been revealed and it is clear that they can never live under the same roof in any sort of peace. After this scene, they do not appear on stage together for the rest of the play.

Nanna may not speak directly to Mena in the remainder of the play, but she does discuss her feelings for her with her son when she tries to convince him not to allow the match between Sive and Seán Dóta. She makes no secret of her loathing for her daughter-in-law, blaming her for the match and telling Mike: 'There was never an ounce of luck in this house since that greasy bitch darkened the door of it.' She goes on to call Mena 'a hungry sow' and 'a pauperised wretch'. Mike is deeply unhappy to be caught between his mother and his wife. Nanna's hatred for Mena does not help her to win Mike over to her point of view about the match. It clouds the issue and leads Mike to complain that Nanna has 'never had a good word' for Mena and that he has 'no rest' from the pair of them. Nanna's attacks on Mena force Mike to take sides and to declare that 'a man's wife will always be his wife, let them both be what they will'.

> She makes no secret of her loathing for her daughter-in-law, blaming her for the match

While we never see Nanna and Mena together again after their vicious fight in Act 1, Scene 3, we can easily imagine the effect that Sive's death will have on the relationship between the pair. Life in the Glavin household will undoubtedly be filled with even more hatred, bitterness, blame and guilt than ever as the two women cope with the tragic aftermath of Mena's plotting to rid herself of her niece and mother-in-law.

Sive and Liam

Sive and Liam love one another dearly. Their relationship contrasts sharply with the other relationships in the play, most of which are

THE COMPARATIVE STUDY: **RELATIONSHIPS**

marked by hatred, scheming, selfishness, greed and lust.

The youngsters are linked by their appearance and by their refinement. The stage directions tell us that Sive is 'a pretty young girl' and Liam is 'good-looking and manly'. Liam's voice is 'cultured' and neither he nor Sive uses the north Kerry vernacular that peppers the speech of the rest of the characters. They speak politely, never rising to the taunts and insults of others. Both are intelligent: Sive attends a convent school and works hard at her studies; and Mike says that Liam possesses 'quick words and book-readin' like all belonging to you'. Sive and Liam belong to a different world than that inhabited by the other characters. They believe in marrying for love and cannot comprehend the idea of matchmaking for money.

The first time we see Liam and Sive together is when Liam drops in to the Glavin house unexpectedly. They speak tenderly and lovingly to one another, and Liam appears devoted to Sive: 'I would marry nobody but you, Sive, I love you.' He risks the wrath of Sive's uncle should he be found in the house, but he doesn't care: 'He might as well hate me as anybody.' Liam is not underhanded and wants his relationship with Sive to be out in the open. When Mike comes home and accuses Liam of 'stealing and sneaking' around like 'a rat when he saw the nest empty', Liam does not rise to the provocation but says calmly that he makes 'no denial' of the fact that he is after Sive. He is brave and fearless in his love for Sive and refuses to be put off by Mike's threats and insults, telling the older man: 'You will not command the lives and happiness of two people who love each other.'

> *'I would marry nobody but you, Sive, I love you'*

Liam's courage and devotion to Sive is admirable, but it is clear that there are several obstacles in the way of their continuing relationship. Mike dislikes and distrusts Liam because it was a relation of his who got Sive's mother pregnant and 'left her with a child with no name'. He fears that Liam will do the same to Sive, and orders him to stay away from the house and from Sive. Mena and Thomasheen have their own reasons for wanting to keep Sive and Liam apart. They plan to marry her off to Seán Dóta, and are determined to keep Sive under tight control lest she slip away to meet Liam.

Sive is still a young girl in her uncle's care, and she fears his anger far more than Liam does. She is anxious lest Mike should catch Liam in the house: 'My uncle Mike … He'll have a fit, Liam!' When Mike enters and finds them together, he immediately sends Sive to her room. She obeys him without protest. Neither has she the strength to stand up to Mena, and it seems inevitable that Mena will eventually succeed in bending Sive to her will. The young girl's goodness, inexperience and naive innocence are no match for the machinations of her scheming aunt.

Liam does his best to prevent the match going ahead. He calls to the house again but Mena refuses to allow him to speak to Sive. Mike appears and is infuriated to find Liam there. He and Mena threaten and insult Liam, but the young man is unmoved. He proves his love for Sive by selflessly offering to leave the area until she is a woman, and begs Mike and Mena not to give Sive to 'that rotting old man with his gloating eyes and trembling hands'. Mike and Mena refuse to listen to Liam's entreaties, and he leaves. When Sive enters, saying she thought she heard Liam's voice, Mena cruelly tells her that he merely called to wish Sive well in her married life and to say that he is leaving for good. Sive is distraught, but even in the midst of her anguish she maintains a belief in Liam's loyalty and love: 'Oh! Liam could never do a thing like that.'

> Sive is distraught, but even in the midst of her anguish she maintains a belief in Liam's loyalty and love

It appears that the relationship between Sive and Liam is doomed, but help comes in the form of Pats Bocock and Carthalawn. Pats is impressed by the love Liam and Sive have for one another, telling Nanna: 'The young man have a true heart for her. She have a true heart for him.' Together with Liam, Pats and Carthalawn devise a plan to get a letter to Sive, telling her that Liam will elope with her that night if she can slip out of the house. The letter is entrusted to Nanna, as she is the only other person who supports the young couple. For the first time in the play, the audience

THE COMPARATIVE STUDY: **RELATIONSHIPS**

is hopeful that perhaps true love will prevail and that Sive and Liam will manage to elope.

Such optimism is short-lived, however. Nanna gives the letter to Mike, asking him to pass it on to Sive. Thomasheen intercepts it and reads it aloud. He scorns the romantic language and the beautiful sentiments Liam expresses. Mike, on the other hand, is moved and impressed by the obvious love and trust that exists in the relationship between Sive and Liam. Liam does not believe that Sive is marrying Seán Dóta of her own free will and promises to wait all night for her to come to him so that they can be married the next morning. Thomasheen grabs the letter and burns it, thereby ensuring an end to Sive and Liam's romance.

> That Sive should die without ever knowing that Liam had a plan to rescue her from her plight is heartbreaking

The relationship between Liam and Sive ends in terrible suffering. Isolated from those who love her, Sive is driven to complete despair. She escapes from the house and runs into the bog where she commits suicide by drowning herself in a bog hole. Liam sees Sive running across the bog but she is so distraught that she does not hear him call her. That Sive should die without ever knowing that Liam had a plan to rescue her from her plight is heartbreaking.

Liam is devastated by Sive's death. He carries her body into the house, water dripping like tears from both him and the dead girl. He rages against Mena, calling her a 'horrible filthy bitch' and accusing her of driving Sive to her death. Lovingly, he dries Sive's hair with a towel while sorrowfully admiring her: 'The beautiful hair of her! The lovely silky white of her!' Our final impression of Liam is of his deep and abiding love for Sive.

THE COMPARATIVE STUDY

Hero/Heroine/Villain

Ordinary Level

Note

In this mode, students may choose a hero **or** heroine **or** villain from their Comparative Study texts.

Past questions on this mode of comparison have tended to focus on the following:

- *Why you find the hero/heroine/villain interesting*
- *Why you like or dislike the hero/heroine/villain*
- *How the hero/heroine/villain contributed to your enjoyment of the text*
- *Why you consider the character to be a hero/heroine/villain*
- *What part the hero/heroine/villain plays in the storyline.*

Hero: Liam Scuab

Liam Scuab is undoubtedly the hero of the text. He is an honourable and loving young man who stands up for what he believes in and refuses to be dragged down to the level of those who oppose him. He conducts himself with dignity and integrity throughout the play and is a thoroughly admirable character.

Our introduction to Liam predisposes us to view him in a good light. The stage directions tell us that he is 'good looking and manly, his voice cultured and refined'. He has called to the Glavin house in the hope of meeting Sive, despite the fact that he is not welcome there. His love for Sive is such that he defies those who would keep them apart. When he speaks to Sive, Liam shows a romantic spirit and a high level of respect for the girl he loves. Sive is not sure if she will be able to get away to meet him later, but Liam loyally says that he will 'wait till the crack of dawn, anyway'. He is steadfast in his love for Sive, saying that he would marry nobody but her. Liam's warmth, kindness and loving nature make him an appealing character.

When Mike comes home suddenly and catches Liam talking to Sive, he responds angrily, ordering Sive to her room and threatening Liam. Mike insultingly accuses Liam of wanting to take advantage of Sive: 'I know what you're looking for', but Liam denies having any dishonourable motive: 'There's no need to sound so dirty about it.' He makes no secret of his love for Sive, and his openness, politeness and decency contrast sharply with Mike's rudeness and coarseness. Later on in the play when he visits the Glavins again and begs Mike and Mena not to go ahead with the match, Liam shows once more how controlled and mannerly he is. In response to verbal insults and threats of physical violence, Liam simply replies, 'I tell you I want no trouble. If I have upset ye, I'm sorry.'

> *'I tell you I want no trouble. If I have upset ye, I'm sorry'*

Liam is a selfless man who wants nothing but the best for Sive. Her happiness is paramount, which is why he offers to 'leave these parts till Sive is a woman' if that will persuade Mike to abandon the idea of a match. Liam begs Mike 'not to give her to that rotting old man with his gloating eyes and trembling hands'. Even Mike is moved by this plea, and his anger abates somewhat in the face of such love and compassion. Liam appeals to both Mike and Mena to consider how morally wrong it is to make such a match for money: 'Forget about yourselves and see it with good eyes instead of greedy ones.' But his pleas fall on deaf ears. Mena is outraged to be asked to think about the implications of making such a match and threatens to take a knife to Liam: 'I'll open you if you vex me more.'

Unfortunately, Liam's goodness and kindness are no match for the evil scheming of Thomasheen and Mena. He does all he can to prevent the marriage, but there are circumstances over which Liam has no control. Mena, Mike and Thomasheen are so consumed with greed that they will not back down from their plan. Nevertheless, Liam persists in his efforts, devising a plan to rescue Sive with the help of Pats and Carthalawn. He writes a beautiful and moving letter to the girl in which he repeats his love for her and says that he believes she is being

THE COMPARATIVE STUDY: **HERO/HEROINE/VILLAIN**

forced into the marriage with Seán Dóta against her will. He offers to wait all night for her in his house and plans to take her to the city to marry her the next morning, if she can get away. This last-ditch attempt to save Sive shows Liam's determination, courage and loyalty. Even Mike is impressed by the obvious sincerity of the letter and by Liam's love for Sive. However, Liam's plan comes to nothing when the letter falls into Thomasheen's hands and is burnt before it reaches Sive.

> When Sive, distraught and in deep despair, takes her own life, it is only Liam who truly grieves for her

When Sive, distraught and in deep despair, takes her own life, it is only Liam who truly grieves for her. His anguish and anger when he carries her body into the house are powerfully moving. He rages against Mena, accusing her of driving Sive to her death and she flees in the face of his passion. Seán Dóta and Thomasheen sneak away in a cowardly fashion while Mike seems to fall apart, babbling about needing a priest. Of the five of them, only Liam shows real sorrow, gently drying Sive's hair and mourning the loss of such a beautiful, innocent girl. He is a true hero, remaining loyal to the love of his life until the end.

Villain: Mena Glavin

Mena Glavin is most certainly a villain. She is a cruel, greedy, amoral, manipulative, vicious woman whose evil plotting ruins the lives of those around her. Her name, which needs only a slight readjustment to spell 'mean', suits her well.

The stage directions which introduce Mena give us an early indication of her personality. She is 'hard-featured' and her black hair is 'tied sharply' in a bun. There is nothing soft or yielding about this woman. When she speaks, this impression is reinforced. She has not a good word to say to Nanna or Sive, but instead harangues them for idleness and for talking while others work.

Mena detests Nanna and shows her none of the respect due to her age and status in the household. She is cruel to the old lady, pointing out that she 'has great gumption for a woman with nothing'. The audience may have some sympathy with Mena early on in the play when she bickers with Nanna, as the old woman is also unpleasant and provocative in her manner, taunting Mena for her poor upbringing and her childlessness. However, as the play progresses, we see that Mena's diabolical treatment of Nanna is out of all proportion to the provocation she receives. Supported by Thomasheen, she threatens to throw Nanna out of her home and even moves to strike her – 'I'll take the head from your shoulders' – but is held back by Thomasheen. Anyone who crosses Mena is instantly subject to a vicious verbal assault and, on a number of occasions, the threat of physical violence. She takes a kitchen knife from the dresser and warns Liam that she will 'open' him if he continues to speak out against the match.

Mena also treats Sive very badly. She resents the girl her education and the affection she receives from Nanna: 'Why should that young rip be sent to a convent every day instead of being out earning with a farmer?' It is clear that this resentment has existed since Sive was a baby as Mena tells Mike that when she married him she had to contend with 'a dirty brat of an orphan bawling in the corner'. Mena's unloving, hard nature is revealed by this comment. She had no sympathy or affection for a small girl who had lost her mother, but instead felt hard done by for having to take her on.

'Why should that young rip be sent to a convent every day instead of being out earning with a farmer'

Neither is Mena's husband, Mike, spared her dislike and contempt. She speaks scornfully of him to Nanna, calling him a 'poor amadawn' who, before their marriage, went around 'like a half-fool'. She also blames Mike for her childlessness, telling Nanna that he is a 'tired gomeril of a man'. Mena is no kinder when speaking directly to Mike. She is civil enough when he does as she asks, but when he stands up to her, she quickly reverts to her harsh, cruel self. Mike refuses to consider allowing Sive to marry Seán Dóta when Mena raises the topic first, and she turns on him contemptuously, calling him a 'man of straw'.

THE COMPARATIVE STUDY: **HERO/HEROINE/VILLAIN**

Mena is an amoral woman who is motivated purely by selfish interests. She will stop at nothing to get what she wants, and what she wants most of all is money. When Thomasheen tells her that Seán Dóta is willing to pay her £200 if she will give him Sive as a bride, the girl's fate is sealed. Mena is determined to do whatever it takes to get that money. Of course, she is also pleased at the thought of being rid of a girl she despises. The fact that Nanna going with Sive is part of the bargain only makes the deal all the sweeter. That Sive does not want to marry Seán Dóta is entirely immaterial. Mena has no concern whatsoever for Sive's happiness, nor is she moved by Mike's comment that to give Sive to Seán Dóta would be 'like tossing the white flower of the canavaun on to the manure heap'.

Mena manages to manipulate Mike until he comes around to her way of thinking, but she has a harder task with Sive. Her ways of persuading the girl to agree to the marriage are monstrously cruel. When her attempts to show Sive the financial benefits of the match come to nothing, Mena drops the kindly attitude she had adopted in an effort to win Sive around, and harshly tells her that her father abandoned her mother and that she is 'a bye-child, a common bye-child – a bastard!' Having shattered Sive's illusions about her parents, Mena goes on to tell her that she is finished with school, flinging Sive's schoolbag across the room as she speaks. As if all of this were not enough, Mena also separates Sive from her confidante and supporter, Nanna. Shrewdly, Mena calculates that if she can isolate Sive and keep her a virtual prisoner in the house, she will break the girl's spirit. Mena's final, and greatest, act of villainy in her manipulation of Sive is to tell her the lie that Liam called to wish her well in her married life and to say that he is emigrating for good. Sive is utterly devastated to hear this, and runs to her room in tears. Mike is unhappy to see his niece so distraught, but Mena is unrepentant: 'There 'tis all settled and no more to it.'

It could be argued that Mena's poverty-stricken upbringing is partly responsible for her hardness and her steely determination to make as much money as she can in order to be independent. When she is trying to convince Sive of the benefits of a match with Seán Dóta, Mena says, 'Will you thank God that you won't be for the rest of your days working for the bare bite and sup like the poor women of the parish.' However, a fear of poverty does not excuse Mena's insistence that Sive go ahead with the match when the girl makes it abundantly clear that she is appalled at the prospect. Mena does not care about Sive and has no real wish to see her well settled. What Mena wants is the money that will come to her when Sive is wed. She even cheats Sive of the money Seán Dóta gave her for wedding clothes.

When Thomasheen brings this up, Mena shows no shame whatsoever, asking: 'Who is better entitled to it than me?'

Mena's heartless, selfish plan appears to be succeeding. Sive's spirit is broken and she no longer has the will to fight. However, all Mena's plotting comes to nothing when, the night before the wedding, Sive slips from the house and drowns herself in a bog hole rather than face marrying Seán Dóta. When the heartbroken Liam carries Sive's body into the house and lays it reverently on the table, we can empathise with his rounding on Mena in furious disgust. Her villainy has destroyed the happiness of those around her and has cost Sive her life. It is hard to argue with Liam when he calls her a 'horrible filthy bitch' and 'a heartless wretch that hunted the poor little girl to her grave'.

> What Mena wants is the money that will come to her when Sive is wed. She even cheats Sive of the money Seán Dóta gave her for wedding clothes

Mena's reaction to Sive's death does little to endear her to us, even when she appears to realise the consequences of her actions. Certainly, she is shocked; her almost numbly disbelieving 'drowned, dead' when she sees her niece's body shows how she struggles to come to terms with the fact by stating it aloud. Still, there is little sense of real grief. We wonder whether her shock is based on sadness and horror at the loss of Sive, or sadness and horror at the loss of her own hopes and dreams for the future. Nothing in Mena's behaviour thus far in the play has given us cause to believe that she may truly mourn the death of her innocent, heartbroken niece, or that she may learn from, and perhaps be bettered by, this dreadful experience. She flees to her room in the face of Liam's accusations, a rather cowardly and undignified reaction to such an appalling outcome to all her scheming and ruthless manipulation. It is difficult to see any redemption in Mena's behaviour at the end of the play, and our final impression of her is that she is a villainous woman who has blighted the lives of those around her.

THE COMPARATIVE STUDY

Aspects of Story: Tension, Climax or Resolution

Ordinary Level

Past questions on this mode of comparison have tended to focus on the following:
- How the tension **or** climax **or** resolution holds your interest in the story being told
- The importance of the tension **or** climax **or** resolution in the text
- A key moment in which the tension **or** climax **or** resolution is clearly shown.

Tension

Sive is fraught with tension. The story of an innocent young girl whose life and happiness is at the mercy of unscrupulous, amoral schemers cannot fail to hold our attention from start to finish. We are swept along as the story unfolds, and we empathise with Sive and Liam Scuab as they struggle desperately to stay together in the face of ferocious opposition.

Even before the ill-fated match between Sive and Seán Dóta is proposed, there is a great deal of tension in the Glavin household. Sive is caught in the middle of the hostile relationship between Nanna and Mena. Mena's resentment of Sive is obvious from the start, and she treats her with angry contempt and bitterness. As Nanna is so fond of pointing out, Mena is from a poor background and is childless. As a result, Mena cannot bear to see her illegitimate niece receiving preferential treatment in the house: 'Why should that young rip be sent to a convent every day instead of being out earning with a farmer?' Sive's education costs money, and Mena bitterly resents this: 'Your uncle and I work ourselves to the marrow of the bones to give you schooling.'

Nanna adores Sive but is not in a position to do much to protect her from Mena's scorn and hatred. It is clear that Mena rules the house with an iron fist and, for all the insults Nanna fires at her, she can do nothing but watch when her daughter-in-law criticises Sive harshly and orders her to her room to study.

When Thomasheen suggests the match between the elderly, wealthy, lecherous Seán Dóta and Sive, Mena is quickly persuaded of the advantages of getting rid of her niece and mother-in-law in one fell stroke while at the same time making a sizeable sum of money from the arrangement. She knows that the girl will be unhappy at the idea, but she doesn't care. Her husband, Mike, is unlikely to agree to it easily, but Thomasheen suggests ways in which she might manipulate both Sive and Mike and force them to go along with the plan. Thomasheen adds greatly to the tension in the play by pitting characters against one another and widening the existing divisions between them. He urges Mena to harass and bully both Sive and Nanna, something she needs little encouragement to do.

> Thomasheen adds greatly to the tension in the play by pitting characters against one another and widening the existing divisions between them

Mike is appalled at the thought of the match, and he and Mena fight bitterly over it. The tension between them increases to the point where Mena jeers at what she perceives as Mike's weakness and lack of masculinity: 'Go away, man of straw.' The stage directions show us the rising hostility between husband and wife. Mike speaks 'harshly' and is 'loud voiced'. When he is taunted beyond endurance, he leaps up 'in a violent fit of temper, he knocks over the chair upon which he had been sitting and goes out, slamming the door'. Mena follows him, calling his name.

No sooner have Mena and Mike left the house than Liam Scuab enters. His arrival is yet another source of tension. Sive expresses alarm lest her uncle catch Liam in the house: 'He'll have a fit, Liam!' Nanna advises them to keep watch, saying that if they are caught together 'there'll be no more peace in this house'. As our impression

THE COMPARATIVE STUDY: ASPECTS OF STORY

of the house so far is that it is certainly not a peaceful place, we wonder how much worse it could get. We soon find out. Mike arrives home and is furious to find Liam there. His language is aggressive and threatening. He hates Liam because it was the young man's cousin who got Sive's mother pregnant. Mike firmly believes that he abandoned her, and will hear no explanation to the contrary, although Liam explains that the man died in an accident but had every intention of marrying Sive's mother. Mike is unimpressed. He makes a dire threat to Liam, saying that if he tries to see Sive again he will 'pay as dear as your cousin paid, maybe'.

The introduction of Seán Dóta to the play makes us see how impossible it is that Sive should marry such a man. The tension in the air is almost palpable from the moment he arrives with Thomasheen. Mike is unhappy but reasonably courteous, while Mena fawns over the elderly farmer. His awkward, unsuccessful attempts to impress Sive are embarrassing and only succeed in showing us how little they have in common. His ridiculous, unsuitable poem portrays him as an uneducated, rather foolish man. Mena is undaunted. She contrives to send him and Sive down the road together on a false errand, and the old man makes an aggressive pass at the girl. Sive is utterly repulsed by this, telling Nanna on her return that he 'nearly tore the coat' off her.

Pats Bocock and his son Carthalawn play an important role in *Sive*. Their appearance heightens the emotional impact of the play, and their commentary on characters and events is accurate and scathing. The rhythm of the bodhrán and the tapping of Pats' stick as they prepare to launch into one of their songs convey the rising tension in the play.

> The rhythm of the bodhrán and the tapping of Pats' stick as they prepare to launch into one of their songs convey the rising tension in the play

Thomasheen loathes the tinkers because they despise him and his mercenary matchmaking. When they leave, Thomasheen vents his fury on Nanna, blaming her for spreading gossip about the match. Mena joins him in his attack on the vulnerable old woman. They are so violent in their speech and body language that we wonder if they will actually do her harm. At one point, Mena goes so far as to raise her hand to strike Nanna, shouting that she will 'take the head from your shoulders'. This is a terribly tense time in that we see just how evil Mena and Thomasheen are, and we fear they will stop at nothing to achieve their ends.

> At one point, Mena goes so far as to raise her hand to strike Nanna, shouting that she will 'take the head from your shoulders'

When Nanna leaves, Thomasheen begins to increase the pressure on Mena to get Sive to agree to the match. He is very keen to hear that Sive has 'said the word out of her mouth'. Spurred on by Thomasheen, Mena tackles Sive almost immediately. As soon as she has the girl alone, she does all she can to break her down and force her to agree to the marriage. Her methods are cruel but effective. Having distressed the girl with a false version of her parents' story, she isolates Sive completely by ending her schooling and forbidding her to share a room with Nanna. The tension here is created by the audience's realisation that Sive's avenues of escape are being closed off one by one. She is like a prey animal separated from its family by a pair of cunning and vicious predators and hounded until she drops.

The only hope we have left is that Liam may yet save the day. He is brave and resolute, and he loves Sive dearly. However, he is no match for the amoral and unscrupulous Mena. She and Mike refuse to listen to his pleas that they reconsider the match, and they throw him out of the house with terrible threats of violence. Mena tells Sive that Liam only called to wish her well in her marriage and to say he is leaving the area for good. This is the final straw for Sive. Distraught – 'Oh! Liam could never do a thing like that' – she flees to her room in tears. It seems that all is lost.

However, our hopes are raised again, only to be dashed almost as quickly, when Liam contrives to have a letter delivered to Nanna. It contains details of a plan for them to elope and the intention is for Nanna to pass it on to Sive. We wonder if she will succeed in doing this in a house filled with suspicion and diabolical scheming. In the event,

THE COMPARATIVE STUDY: ASPECTS OF STORY

she does not. The tension surrounding the letter is almost unbearable. Mike takes it from Nanna, promising to pass it to Sive. He is clearly unsure about the wisdom of doing this, and we can only hope that he will do so and thus save Sive from a life of misery.

Thomasheen's sudden entry and his spotting of Mike's secreting the letter in his pocket marks the end of our hopes. He forces Mike to read it aloud, then snatches it and burns it. As the letter goes up in smoke, so does Sive's last chance of happiness.

Climax

The moment of greatest tension in *Sive* occurs on the night before the wedding. Sive is utterly dejected and defeated. She has lost all her spirit and refuses offers of food and drink, claiming her head is 'on fire'. She leaves the others to their pre-wedding celebration, and goes to her room.

Thomasheen, Mike and Mena are joined by Seán Dóta. He is in high spirits, looking forward to his impending marriage. It seems that nothing can stop the wedding now. Pats and Carthalawn arrive, ostensibly to offer their blessings on the wedding. They arranged this visit earlier with Nanna, in the belief that their calling would allay any suspicions and reassure the others that all was well. As always, the tinkers bring tension with them to the Glavin house. Their blessing on Seán Dóta soon turns to a curse, and Carthalawn says, 'Now I swear upon this verse/He'll be travelling soon by hearse/And we'll never see Seán Dóta anymore.'

> *'There's a bundle of clothes under the quilt where she should be lying. She's after stealing away on us!'*

At that moment Mena, who had gone to fetch Sive to please Seán Dóta, starts to call hysterically that Sive has gone: 'There's a bundle of clothes under the quilt where she should be lying. She's after stealing away on us!' Her news throws the house into uproar. Thomasheen hopes she has merely gone in to see Nanna, but a quick check reveals this not to be the case. Mena is bewildered, wondering where Sive could have gone without 'even a shoe for her feet'.

Now Carthalawn speaks, saying, 'I thought I saw the figure of a girl flashing across the bog near the end of the cutaway where the deep holes do be.' His words strike fear into the hearts of the listeners. The mention of 'the deep holes' is ominous and we too fear for Sive.

Mena is terrified. The stage directions and the dialogue show how panicked she is. She 'shrieks at Mike' and she urges him to hurry: 'What if she fell into a hole … Oh, my God! Find her! Find her! … Hurry yourself!'

Mike rushes to the stable and returns with a lamp and rubber waders, which he hurriedly pulls on. The waders strike fear into the heart of the audience. If, as Mike and Mena said, Sive is out in the bog 'without a shoe or a coat', when a strong man like Mike believes waders and a lamp are necessary, Sive must be in great danger.

> Events have unfolded with alarming speed, and the audience is on tenterhooks, wondering what can have happened to the poor, unfortunate girl

Thomasheen and Seán Dóta offer to accompany Mike, but Mena is so distraught that she refuses to be left alone, and begs Seán Dóta to stay with her.

Events have unfolded with alarming speed, and the audience is on tenterhooks, wondering what can have happened to the poor, unfortunate girl.

Resolution

Just as the men prepare to leave the house to search for Sive, a 'frantic voice' is heard outside. It is Liam. He calls for light, saying that he is coming across the bog towards the house. His tone strikes fear into the hearts of those waiting in the kitchen: 'All exchange frightened glances.'

The hysterical shouting and action of the last few moments is over, and there is a shocked and horrified silence as Liam enters, carrying Sive's dead body in his arms. Water drips from both of them, like tears. Without looking at any of them, Liam walks towards the table, which is

THE COMPARATIVE STUDY: ASPECTS OF STORY

centre stage. His position on stage, facing the audience with the dead girl in his arms, is most dramatic and would undoubtedly make a strong impression on the audience. The silence of the other characters intensifies the horror of the moment. There is no movement, no distraction from the dreadful sight of 'the slight body [hanging] limp in Liam's arms. The silence and the stillness are suddenly broken by Pats. He moves forward and in a dramatic gesture raises his stick and sweeps the table clean'. The ware crashes to the floor. The effect of this on an audience would be quite shocking. The smashing of the plates and cups echoes the shattered hopes and dreams of the characters.

Liam calls for a cloth to dry Sive's hair. As Mena hands him one, Thomasheen and Seán Dóta leave without saying a word. The stage directions tell us how despicable and cowardly their behaviour appears. Thomasheen 'edges slyly' and 'furtively' towards the door, with Seán Dóta 'backing, sneaking' after him.

> Thomasheen 'edges slyly' and 'furtively' towards the door, with Seán Dóta 'backing, sneaking' after him

Liam tells the remaining characters that he saw Sive running across the bog 'and she letting cries out of her that would rend your heart'. He says that she was too distraught to hear his calls for her to stop, and he could not catch her in time to stop her from drowning herself in a deep pool.

Mena seems not to be able to fully comprehend what has happened. In shock, she says, 'Drowned, dead.' At this Liam rounds on her, 'blazing with anger'. He shouts, 'You killed her! You ... you ... you ... killed her! You horrible filthy bitch!' That it should be the hitherto composed and unfailingly polite Liam Scuab who denounces Mena in this way lends great force to his words. He shrieks at Mena to get away from Sive's body, saying that her very presence is 'polluting the pure spirit of the child'. Again, in a most uncharacteristically aggressive move, Liam raises his fist to strike Mena. She flees to her room, shocked and terrified by what has happened, and by Liam's accusing and threatening manner.

Liam's tender love for Sive is shown when he carefully dries her hair with the cloth while mourning her loss: 'The beautiful hair of her!' He takes her dead hand in grief and despair. Even in death, Sive is beautiful to him: 'The lovely silky white of her!'

Mike is completely broken by Sive's death and, presumably, by the realisation that he has to share the responsibility for it. He babbles about needing to get a priest so that Sive can be 'buried in holy ground', but he will not go alone. Pathetically, he begs Liam to go with him: 'There's no luck in going for a priest alone.' What luck Mike thinks he will ever have again after the events of this night is not clear. He is making no sense.

Angrily, Liam drags Mike towards the door and they leave together. Alone with the body of the dead girl, Pats and Carthalawn sing a final song. It is a lament for Sive and it points the finger of blame for her death at those who hounded her into a match against her will:

Oh, they murdered lovely Sive,

She would not be a bride,

And they laid her dead, to bury in the clay.

They leave quietly, still singing their sad song.

The final, heartbreaking image is of Nanna Glavin coming slowly from her room to where Sive's body is lying, and weeping silently over her beloved grandchild. There could hardly be a more affecting end to this tragic tale.

glossary

Abstractedly:	deep in thought, preoccupied with something else
Accoutrements:	accessories, something extra that is not needed but is used for decoration
Achree:	love or darling *(a chroí)*
Adroit:	showing skill or cleverness in handling situations
Airly:	early
Aisy:	easy
Alluding:	referring to something, but not directly
Amadawn:	fool or idiot *(amadán)*
Archly:	mischievously, playfully sly
Aspersions:	slanderous, damaging or unfavourable remarks
Bad skewer:	bad luck
Bane of cows:	a large herd of cattle
Bawdy:	humorously vulgar
Bean a'tighe:	woman of the house *(bean an tí)*
Befuddled:	confused or bewildered
Bell-rag:	humiliate, hold up to scorn
Beyant:	beyond
Blather:	nonsensical talk
Bocock:	beggar or cripple
Bogdeal:	bog deal: pine wood preserved in bogs
Bohareen:	narrow, rural road – usually unpaved *(bóithrín)*
Bonham:	piglet *(banbh)*
Bornack:	limpet: small shellfish that clings tightly to rocks
Bostoon:	clumsy fool

Note

The words/terms in this glossary are only explained in the context in which they appear in Sive. *Fuller definitions and examples of other usages can be found in any good dictionary.*

Where a word derives from an Irish Gaelic word or phrase, the original is also given in brackets

Buachaill:	boy *(buachaill)*
Bualam ski:	foolish talk, boasting *(buaileam sciath)*
Buck:	high-spirited young man
Buttermilk:	the thin milk that is left behind when the butter has been churned out of cream
Bye-child:	a derogatory term for a child born to unmarried parents
Cajolingly:	insincerely flattering or pleading in order to obtain a desired end
Canavaun:	a white, fluffy wild-flower that grows in bogs; also known as bog cotton *(ceannabhán)*
Clane:	clean
Cnabshealing:	whining or complaining *(bheith ag cnáimhseáil)*
Cohackling:	plotting or scheming
Coif:	tight skullcap, similar to the type nuns sometimes wear under their veils. In *Sive*, Mena's hair is pulled back so severely that it resembles a close-fitting cap
Consumptive:	suffering from tuberculosis – a disease of the lungs
Craw:	stomach
Cumar:	deep, steep-sided valley, usually with a stream at the bottom
Curam:	responsibility *(cúram)*
Curran'y cake:	curranty cake
Dacent:	decent
Dartois:	small, light pastry with sweet filling
Deprecating:	disapproving, belittling
Diggle:	devil
Doodeen:	small clay pipe *(dúidín)*

GLOSSARY

Dorn:	fistful or handful *(dorn)*
Dowry:	money or property that a bride brings with her to her marriage. Usually the parents of the girl would provide the dowry to enable their daughter to marry into a good family. The dowry system was part of the matchmaking process, a process which had all but died out in Ireland at the time *Sive* was written
Dul amú:	to go astray or be mistaken. In this context, someone who misses the point/an idiot *(dul amú)*
Dusteen:	little dusting of …
Faix:	faith
Faldals:	little fancy bits and pieces
Fettle:	emotional state/spirits
Folly:	follow
Fricassée:	meat stew
Frieze overcoat:	heavy, woollen coat
Fuastar:	fuss, rush *(fuadar)*
Gainsay:	deny or contradict
Gall:	nerve, insolence
Gibble:	rag *(giobal)*
Gleann na nGealt:	valley in County Kerry known as 'Valley of the Mad' because of a belief that a holy well there cured insanity
Gloatingly:	delighting in a rival's misfortune
Go mbeirimid beo:	shortened version of a wish or a toast meaning 'May we all be alive again at this time next year' *(go mbeirimid beo ar an am seo arís)*
Goadin':	goading: trying to make someone do something that they do not want to do
Gomaill/gomeril:	annoying or foolish person
Gorsoon:	boy *(garsún)*
Gradhbhar:	loving, warm, endearing *(grámhar)*
Guilefully:	deceitfully cunning
Hould your hoult:	hold on a minute
Huist:	be quiet *(éist do bhéal)*
Jinnet:	donkey mare

Ketching:	catching
Leanav:	child *(leanbh)*
Lurgadawn:	useless person
Mate:	meat
Meal:	coarsely ground grain
Moryeah:	as if: an expression that indicates disbelief or hints that someone is faking something, pretence *(mar dhea)*
Muller:	pot
Nate:	neat
Oinseach:	foolish old woman *(óinseach)*
Pauperised:	made very poor, like a pauper
Phuca:	mischievous spirit or hobgoblin *(púca)*
Plinty:	plenty
Pratey:	potato *(práta)*
Quandary:	difficult situation/dilemma
Rameish:	nonsense *(ráiméis)*
Rann:	verse *(rann)*
Sanctimoniously:	with hypocritical righteousness or piety
Sha:	yes *(sea)*
Skillet:	pan
Smohawnach:	prolonged
Snuff:	finely ground tobacco that can be inhaled through the nose
Sonorous:	having a deep, rich, full sound
Sotto voce:	in a low voice
Stentorian:	extremely loud
Sugan chair:	wooden kitchen chair with a woven seat *(súgán)*
Supplicating:	humbly requesting
Tamaill:	[in a] while *(tamaill)*
Tathaire:	scrounger/person who hangs around hoping for favours
Tay:	tea
Tetter:	any skin eruption such as blisters or eczema
Timorously:	apprehensively/fearfully
Tinker:	common name for Travelling people in the 1950s, the word comes from their occupation as tinsmiths

nifty notes

FOR LEAVING CERTIFICATE ENGLISH TEXTS
ORDINARY AND HIGHER LEVEL

Other titles available in the series

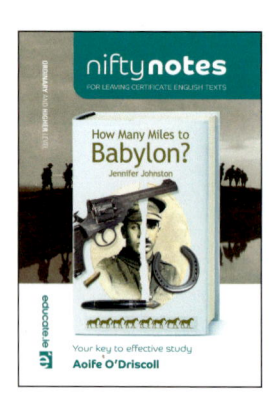

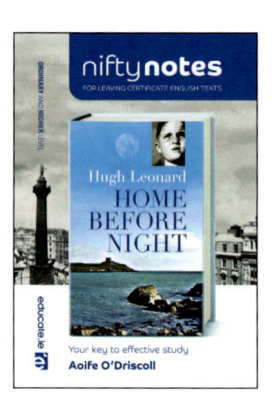

How Many Miles to Babylon?
by Jennifer Johnston

Home Before Night
by Hugh Leonard

educate.ie
Castleisland, Co. Kerry, Ireland
www.educate.ie